More Catholic Than the Pope:

AN INSIDE LOOK AT EXTREME TRADITIONALISM

More Catholic Than the Pope:

An Inside Look at Extreme Traditionalism

Patrick Madrid
and Pete Vere

Our Sunday Visitor Publishing Division
Our Sunday Visitor, Inc.
Huntington, Indiana 46750

To the blessed memory of Pope St. Pius X,

a wise shepherd

and stalwart defender of the Church.

DO NOT ALLOW YOURSELVES to be deceived by the cunning statements of those who persistently claim to wish to be with the Church, to love the Church, to fight so that people do not leave Her ... But judge them by their works. If they despise the shepherds of the Church and even the Pope, if they attempt all means of evading their authority in order to elude their directives and judgments ..., then about which Church do these men mean to speak? Certainly not about that [one] "built upon the foundation of the apostles and prophets, Christ Jesus himself being the cornerstone" (Ephesians 2:20).

— POPE ST. PIUS X (MAY 10, 1909)

Contents

Introduction

What Do We Mean by "More Catholic Than the Pope"?

This book examines the claims made by the extreme-traditionalist movement spawned by the late Archbishop Marcel Lefebvre — the Society of St. Pius X, commonly referred to as the SSPX.[1] At the heart of this story is the question of schism: Is the SSPX separated from the Catholic Church, or is it, as its adherents claim, the most faithful and authentic expression of the Church?

Our thesis is that the SSPX is in schism, and this book will lay out the evidence in support of that conclusion. Along the way, we will consider and respond to various arguments and controversies raised by followers of Archbishop Lefebvre.

A book that questions and critiques, much less indicts, the SSPX and labels it and its followers as "more Catholic than the Pope" is likely to raise a few eyebrows and more than a few tempers. The title of this book is, to be sure, a double entendre and will be understood in two ways.

The authors intend the appellation "more Catholic than the Pope" as a criticism, a fraternal rebuke of Catholics who seem to have lost their way and have arrogated to themselves the position of being the "true defenders" of Holy Tradition, over against the Pope and his predecessor, Pope Paul VI, who, they allege, permitted much of Holy Tradition to slip from their grasp in the wake of Vatican II.

Defenders of extreme traditionalism, including those who have become ensnared within the SSPX's schismatic mindset and activities, will no doubt see being "more Catholic than the Pope" as a good thing! After all, they may retort, "Pope John Paul II has *departed* from authentic Catholic Tradition in key ways, so it is we who are upholding Tradition and, under these circumstances, we rightly deserve (and are even proud of) the status of being 'more Catholic than the Pope.'"

In addressing the problem of schismatic or extreme traditionalism, it is the sincere wish of the authors that the hope expressed by Cardinal Ratzinger will come to pass: "If we manage to show and live the totality of Catholicism in these respects, we may well hope that the schism of Msgr. Lefebvre will not last long."[2]

The difficulty for those of us who are Catholics faithful to the Church's teaching magisterium is that the followers of the many traditionalist schisms that arose after the Second Vatican Council are filled with devotion to the Blessed Mother, extremely conservative with regard to most moral issues afflicting the Western world today, and quite reverent before the Blessed Sacrament during their Latin liturgies. These individuals — at least on the surface — appear to be devout though disaffected Catholics. For this reason, it is easy to sympathize with them.

Nonetheless, it is our hope that the evidence we present in this book will help extreme traditionalists to see the mistakes made by the SSPX and similar groups, and to abandon them and come home to the Church.

Background to the Controversy

Since he illicitly consecrated four new bishops in 1988, in defiance of Pope John Paul II, Archbishop Lefebvre's movement, the Society of St. Pius X, or SSPX, has made strenuous efforts to capture the attention and loyalties of Catholics who are disheartened and disaffected by the liturgical abuses and doctrinal fuzziness that has existed in many parishes. SSPX priests establish autonomous "chapels" in various communities where they celebrate Mass and the sacraments only according to the pre-Vatican II Latin rites.

Some, like the SSPX, claim to be in communion with the Pope and the Church, though they are extremely critical of both. Others, under the banner of sedevacantism,[3] sedeprivationism,[4] or even, in the most extreme of cases, their own so-called popes, claim Pope John Paul II to be an anti-pope. While in no way exhaustive, the aim of this book is to try to shed more light on the vexing controversy surrounding many of the extreme traditional Catholic organizations that have arisen after Vatican II. Are they in schism or not in schism?

Adherents of the SSPX claim to be in communion with the Pope and the Church, even while being extremely critical of both. Critics of the SSPX, including the Pope, point out that, according to canon law, Archbishop Lefebvre's willful defiance of the Roman Pontiff constituted a "schismatic act."

In this book, we will analyze the canonical arguments for the legitimacy and lawfulness of the SSPX that typically accompany this group's harsh criticisms of Pope John Paul II and the so-called "conciliar Church" it despises so deeply. Does the SSPX have a viable case? According to Church history, canon law, and common sense, the answer is a resounding "No!" — and we will attempt to demonstrate this in these pages.

A further aim of this book is to shed more light on the vexing controversy over the broader canonical status of the SSPX and its adherents. Is the group in schism? Is it not in schism? We realize that this controversy won't be resolved easily, nor are we so naïve as to imagine that a single book can settle the issue definitively. Our goal is to try to move the discussion forward a bit by introducing more evidence presented for a popular audience. Resolving the problem is important for many reasons, not the least of which is the Holy Father's publicly expressed concern for the spiritual welfare of the adherents of the SSPX and the overall health of the Body of Christ. Sadly, lay Catholics are being lured out of their parishes and infected with the group's virulent anti-Pope John Paul II, anti-"conciliar Church," anti-Vatican II mindset.

As an example of their mindset, consider this. The official website of the Society of St. Pius X contains this odd assertion: "The Society of St. Pius X professes filial devotion and loyalty to Pope John Paul II, the Successor of St. Peter and the Vicar of Christ. The priests of the society pray for His Holiness and the local ordinary at every Mass they celebrate." This is odd because it clashes so dramatically with their actions and rhetoric.

While it's good to know that the Pope and the bishops in communion with him are being prayed for at SSPX Masses, it's disturbing to see the strange disconnect that exists in the minds of the SSPX adherents. On one hand they profess "filial devotion and loyalty" to the Pope. On the other, they flatly refuse to obey him.

The fact is, Archbishop Lefebvre committed a schismatic act when he illicitly consecrated four new bishops against the will of Pope John Paul II, who had expressly forbidden him to do so. SSPX adherents argue that Archbishop Lefebvre did not go into schism through his disobedience to the Pope because he had just and lawful reasons for defying the Pope. This claim makes one wonder, then, what the SSPX means when it proclaims its "filial devotion and loyalty" to the Pope.

Does the Pope think the society is showing him "filial devotion and loyalty"? Consider this excerpt from Pope John Paul II's apostolic letter, *Ecclesia Dei*:

> In itself this act [of consecrating those four bishops] was one of disobedience to the Roman Pontiff in a very grave matter and of supreme importance for the unity of the Church, such as is the ordination of bishops whereby the apostolic succession is sacramentally perpetuated. Hence, such disobedience — which implies in practice the rejection of the Roman primacy — constitutes a schismatic act [*Code of Canon Law*, 751]. In performing such an act, notwithstanding the formal canonical warning sent to them by the cardinal prefect of the Congregation for Bishops last June 17, Archbishop Lefebvre and the priests Bernard Fellay, Bernard Tissier de Mallerais, Richard Williamson, and Alfonso de Galarreta have incurred the grave penalty of excommunication envisaged by ecclesiastical law [Cf. *Code of Canon Law*, 1382].

Later in the same apostolic letter, the Pope speaks directly to those Catholics who are part of the SSPX or who are tempted to become part of it. Notice the grave urgency of his exhortation:

> In the present circumstances I wish especially to make an appeal both solemn and heartfelt, paternal and fraternal, to all those who until now have been linked in various ways

to the movement of Archbishop Lefebvre, that they may fulfill the grave duty of remaining united to the vicar of Christ
in the unity of the Catholic Church and of ceasing their support in any way for that movement. *Everyone should be aware
that formal adherence to the schism is a grave offense against
God and carries the penalty of excommunication decreed by the
Church's law* [Emphasis added; cf. *Code of Canon Law*,
1364].

In the aftermath of Archbishop Lefebvre's fateful decision,
the SSPX has argued that, according to canon law, it is not
technically in schism but remains a Catholic group in good
standing. Indeed, canon law has been a prime weapon in the
group's attempts to portray itself as licit. Since most lay
Catholics have at best a meager understanding of canon law,
they typically don't have the tools necessary to adequately analyze and evaluate the various claims and charges made by members of the SSPX. To help people sort it all out, this book will
outline the basic canonical and historical arguments raised by
the SSPX and show why they simply don't hold water.

Many who find themselves drawn into extreme traditionalism have been scandalized by abuses in doctrine and liturgy
at their local parish. These abuses plague some Catholic
parishes and dioceses in North America, as well as in Europe
and elsewhere. In fact, it was precisely because of such sympa-
thies, as well as the beauty of the Tridentine Mass, that one of
the present authors found himself frequenting a schismatic traditionalist chapel during his late teens and early twenties. Like
most adherents to this particular traditionalist schism, at the
time he did not believe himself to be spiritually separated from
Rome; and he felt that his canonical separation from Rome was
merely temporary.

Nevertheless, over a decade later this schism still has not reconciled with the Catholic Church. In fact, time has witnessed many attitudes harden and what initially was dismissed as merely a temporary situation has now become normative. So while the current adherents to this schism may still believe they are Catholic, barring a miraculous and massive softening of the heart, their grandchildren will know that they are not. To paraphrase Stephen Hand in his monograph explaining his own journey from extreme traditionalism back to the Catholic Church, all schismatics have accused the Church and the Roman Pontiff of heresy.

At the root of every schism, as the present *Code of Canon Law* explains, "is the withdrawal of submission to the Supreme Pontiff or from communion with the members of the Church subject to him" (Canon 751). Such ruptures from communion with the Church, the *Catechism of the Catholic Church* points out, "wound the unity of Christ's Body" (CCC, 817).[5] For that reason, at the heart of any apologetic and spiritual journey back to full communion with Rome lie many questions about the unity of the Church as an institution founded by Christ.

PART ONE

A Detailed Look at
a Traditionalist Sect:
The Society of St. Pius X

CHAPTER ONE

Before Schism:
What Led to the Founding of the SSPX?

WE ARE NOT BAPTIZED into the hierarchy; do not receive the cardinals sacramentally; will not spend an eternity in the beatific vision of the Pope. Christ is the point. I, myself, admire the present Pope, but even if I criticized him as harshly as some do, even if his successor proved to be as bad as some of those who have gone before, even if I find the Church, as I have to live with it, a pain in the neck, I should still say that nothing that a Pope (or a priest) could do or say would make me wish to leave the Church, although I might well wish that they *would leave.*

— FRANK SHEED

The History of the Movement

To understand the extreme traditionalist movement, one must first understand the history of its prime architect and figurehead, the late Archbishop Marcel Lefebvre.

In the aftermath of the Second Vatican Council, the archbishop served as a key figure in uniting a fragmented traditionalist

Catholic resistance to the theme of *aggiornamento* (updating) that was gaining traction among many bishops. From Archbishop Lefebvre's vantage point, efforts to bring *aggiornamento* to the Church's customs and its approach to the modern world contained within themselves the seeds of the modernist heresy.

He believed the modernizing winds that had begun to blow within the Church would do more than simply update things. They would damage or even obliterate aspects of Tradition with the wrecking ball of modernism. In this, Catholics can sympathize and agree with the archbishop's concerns. It is a sad fact that since Vatican II horrendous abuses and deformations of Catholic Tradition — especially liturgical Tradition — have exploded onto the scene. To deplore abuse and to work to correct it are worthy acts, as a recent Vatican document has itself emphasized, but the question remains: Did Archbishop Lefebvre choose the right path in his quest to counter the problems he saw arising in the Church? It is from the archbishop's movement that many of the other branches of the traditionalist movement sprung, regardless of whether these other movements would move further into schism or return to the bosom of the Church.

On June 15, 1988, having recently broken off negotiations with the Vatican, Archbishop Lefebvre gathered with the secular and religious media at his international seminary in Ecône, Switzerland. After years of difficult relations with the Holy See, the archbishop had finally come to a decision. Facing the crowd, he publicly introduced four priests of his Priestly Society of St. Pius X, or SSPX. The archbishop had previously founded the SSPX in reaction to the various reforms brought about by the Second Vatican Council. Notwithstanding Pope John Paul II's objections, Archbishop Lefebvre introduced these four priests as candidates whom the archbishop intended to consecrate to the episcopacy come June 30, 1988.

Upon hearing the archbishop's public announcement, Cardinal Bernardin Gantin, Prefect for the Congregation of Bishops, issued a formal canonical warning to Lefebvre not to proceed with the threatened episcopal consecrations without papal mandate. Cardinal Gantin warned Archbishop Lefebvre that should he proceed with this course of events, the Holy See would interpret the unlawful episcopal consecrations as an act of schism.[6] On the eve of the proposed date, Cardinal Joseph Ratzinger also followed up with a telegram urging Archbishop Lefebvre not to proceed with his intended episcopal consecrations, requesting the archbishop to return to Rome instead and resume negotiations.[7]

Unfortunately, Archbishop Lefebvre ignored both the telegram and the formal canonical warning it contained, and as one former SSPX seminarian describes what unfolded, "the archbishop consummated the rupture by the illegal ordination of four bishops at Ecône on June 30, 1988, in the presence of an unusually immense throng of the faithful. He was assisted in the act by His Excellency Antonio de Castro Mayer, retired bishop of Campos, Brazil."[8]

Defiant in their belief that the Second Vatican Council was undermining the Church's traditional faith and practices, Archbishop Lefebvre and his followers had come to believe in the existence of a grave crisis infecting the Church. Moreover, they felt that this grave crisis, whether real or imagined, necessitated the illicit consecration of bishops. Among those present for the episcopal consecrations, Bishop Antonio de Castro Mayer summarized the belief in an impending ecclesiastical apocalypse being averted through Lefebvre's actions. Here is a telling excerpt:

This is the situation in which we find ourselves. We live in an unprecedented crisis in the Church, a crisis which touches it in its essence, in its substance even, which is the holy Sacrifice of the Mass and the Catholic priesthood, the two mysteries essentially united, because without the holy priesthood there is no holy Sacrifice of the Mass, and by consequence, no form of public worship whatsoever ...

Because of this, since the conservation of the priesthood and of the Holy Mass is at stake, and in spite of the requests and the pressure brought to bear by many, I am here to accomplish my duty: to make a public profession of faith.[9]

Thus, the Holy Father faced an obstinate refusal on the part of Archbishop Lefebvre and the SSPX to submit to his authority as Roman Pontiff. This refusal culminated in the illicit consecration of four SSPX priests to the episcopate. On July 2, 1988, after carefully weighing his options, Pope John Paul II made the difficult decision to declare Archbishop Lefebvre, the four bishops illicitly consecrated by him, and those who adhere to Lefebvre's movement to be in schism. Furthermore, he legislated various options to provide for the needs of the faithful who wished to preserve the old Latin Liturgy in full communion with Rome.

Sadly, Archbishop Lefebvre passed away in Ecône in March of 1991 without formally reconciling either his followers or himself with the Church. Bishop de Castro Mayer passed away a month later in Campos, Brazil. Bishop de Castro Mayer's successor would lead his followers back into full communion with Rome within ten years of the bishop's death, and today his followers enjoy their own juridical structure within the Church which is known as the Apostolic Administration of St. John Vianney. Yet, similar negotiations with Archbishop Lefebvre's followers broke down, and today the SSPX remains in a state of schism from the Catholic Church. The most recent statistics number their priests at approximately four hundred and fifty, with a presence on five continents. Many estimates place the number of adherents to Archbishop Lefebvre's schism at the one million mark.

Who Was Archbishop Marcel Lefebvre?

No schism arises in a vacuum. Nor, in the Church's colorful 2000-year history, has a schism ever appeared suddenly. More often than not, they arise over time. Archbishop Lefebvre's traditionalist schism is no different in this regard; it was the culmination of a growing separation between Rome and Ecône, where the SSPX was headquartered. Yet relative to most other major schisms that have wounded the Church in her two-thousand-year history, Lefebvre's schism is relatively recent. Thus the history of the SSPX schism remains clouded with emotion as many of its instrumental players are still alive and as defining events of the life of this schism continue to unfold.

Yet life was not always so complicated for Archbishop Lefebvre. The archbishop came from a good French Catholic home. By all accounts his mother Gabrielle Lefebvre (maiden name: Watine) was a holy woman, an alleged stigmatic,[10] and a dedicated Third Order Franciscan. In fact, up until her son began to run into difficulties with the Church hierarchy, her cause was being investigated for beatification. Thus the Catholic Faith always played a central role in Marcel Lefebvre's upbringing. Few were surprised when, as a young man, he discerned a calling to the priesthood.

Once ordained a Spiritan Missionary, he quickly found himself dispatched to French-speaking Africa. Here he helped establish several dioceses and later became the founding Archbishop of Dakar, Senegal. He continued to found more missionary dioceses in French-speaking Africa. He was eventually appointed by Pope Pius XII to be papal legate to French-speaking Africa. Before retiring in Rome just after the Second Vatican Council, the archbishop also served as superior general for the Spiritan Missionaries.

Confusion in the French Seminaries

The actual history of the SSPX begins around the time of the Second Vatican Council. Certain problems arose within the French seminaries during this time, and many young seminarians became disenchanted by the confusion and contradictory messages that appeared within their formation. At the French seminary in Rome named Santa Chiara, the archbishop was introduced to a young seminarian named Paul Aulagnier and several of his fellow seminarians. In an interview with Luc Gagnon for the conservative Catholic newspaper *The Wanderer*, Father Aulagnier recalls this introduction as follows:

We were in the midst of the Second Vatican Council in 1964. The seminarians followed, as much as they could, this ecclesiastical event. All was on fire — the Church, perhaps; the seminary, for sure. More than 50 French bishops were staying at the seminary. Father Congar was among us.

The directors of the seminary often invited such and such a conciliar father to a spiritual conference each evening. They were of every tendency. It certainly brought some of us joy to hear Archbishop Lefebvre on the two or three occasions he was invited. Differing from the others, he spoke little about the Council. Rather he spoke about the priesthood to which we desired ordination. Like several of my fellow seminarians, I appreciated his presentation of the Catholic priesthood.

As time passed, this small group of French seminarians became increasingly concerned about what was happening around them. Father Aulagnier relates:

> In a university seminary, minds react quickly, undergo influences, and seek to understand. One participated at the seminary in all the systematic changes of everything — of the common life, of the house rules, of theology, of scholastics. In the midst of this spiritual and intellectual agitation, we needed to be careful, to reflect, to inquire, and to read a lot in order to remain informed.
>
> Our little group of traditional seminarians saw themselves quickly becoming the object of criticisms by the direction. When many of us in our year of theology, we are in 1968 now, made our demand for the tonsure, to become a cleric, we were refused. It was then that we resolutely turned towards Archbishop Lefebvre.

Some of the seminarians went off to study with Father Theodosios — a priest ordained by the archbishop's close friend Cardinal Siri — while others decided to wait out their seminary formation with the French seminary in Rome.

The Seminarians Approach the Archbishop

By 1969, things had become intolerable within many French seminaries as young men of a more orthodox persuasion found themselves drummed out and excluded from the seminary. As one former seminary professor who remembers that era told one of the present authors off the record, "It was sad if you want to know the truth. More than any others, the French took modernization further than what the conciliar fathers had intended at the Second Vatican Council. They admitted open Communists to their seminaries, but often there was no room at the inn for young men seeking to live a life of service and prayer."

Feeling abandoned amidst the numerous changes, Paul Aulagnier and eight of his fellow seminarians banded together and approached Archbishop Lefebvre. "I was part of the first nine seminarians of Archbishop Lefebvre," Father Aulagnier shares. "One day in September of 1969, after having arranged my affairs in Rome, I told the superior of the seminary my reasons for leaving, and obtained from my diocesan bishop the authorization to pass from Rome to Fribourg ... Being in some way the oldest [seminarian] and having already had four years of seminary gave me the opportunity to speak often with Archbishop Lefebvre."

As the oldest seminarian among the archbishop's first class, Aulagnier became quite close to Archbishop Lefebvre. Father Aulagnier reports that the two often went for long walks together where the archbishop would share various stories about his time as a missionary in Africa, his future plans for the Society of St. Pius X, and his concerns about what was happening in the Church in the aftermath of the Second Vatican Council. Father Aulagnier spent a lot of time simply observing and listening to the archbishop, and thus he was quite familiar with Archbishop Lefebvre's mindset during this period of time.

Concerning what drove Archbishop Lefebvre, Father Aulagnier explains:

> Here is the great preoccupation of Msgr. Lefebvre. Here is what explains the whole of Msgr. Lefebvre. He feared — he believed — that the spirit of the Reform was going to corrupt Catholic thinking. In every department — whether

liturgical, philosophical, theological, political — he was horrified by "the modern world," considered in its essence; by a revolutionary world, born in 1789.

He saw there an influence that was leading many towards a Lutheran mindset. He hated this revolutionary spirit that refused subjection, submission, subordination to a created order, to a divine order. He was horrified by a "free thinking" that was Protestant, Masonic, characteristic of the modern world and which inspires all of modern thinking. He was horrified by philosophical and political liberalism. For it marched against the social royalty of our Lord Jesus Christ.

There was no doubt: The thinking of Archbishop Lefebvre had been formed by the thinking of the Popes of the nineteenth and twentieth centuries — Pius IX, Leo XIII, St. Pius X, Pius XII — these were his masters. From there springs his love for the Catholic Church founded upon Peter by our Lord Jesus Christ. From there springs his love of Catholic doctrine, of her dogmas, and of her moral laws. For Archbishop Lefebvre, God as Trinity is everything. It is the royal road of the Church and of every baptized person.

CHAPTER TWO

The Rise and Fall of the SSPX Within the Catholic Church

THE LINE, OFTEN ADOPTED by strong men in controversy, [is] of justifying the means by the end.
— ST. JEROME (A.D. 342-420), *LETTER 48*

The Creation of the Society of St. Pius X

In October of 1970, Archbishop Lefebvre received permission from Bishop Nestor Adam of Sion, Switzerland, to found a religious institute with a central house of studies in Ecône, Switzerland. Lefebvre, as Father Oppenheimer explains, "did this at the instigation of a number of young seminarians who had sought him out for an authentic priestly formation during that time of confusion in the Church."[11] The archbishop would always maintain that he never sought to recruit these seminarians — rather the seminarians were the ones to approach him. Regardless of whether or not this claim is factually correct — and there is nothing to suggest otherwise —

it helped cement Archbishop Lefebvre's mystique among his followers.

It was in light of this background that the archbishop and his first class of seminarians obtained permission from François Charrière, the diocesan bishop of Lausanne, Geneva, and Fribourg to found the SSPX as some form of ecclesiastical entity. Nevertheless, the canonical nature of this entity remains disputed. Those favorable to the SSPX claim their priestly society of common life without vows was founded in accordance with Canons 673-674, and 488, Nos. 3 and 4, of the 1917 *Code of Canon Law,* which was then in effect.[12]

Nevertheless, if one carefully examines the decree establishing the SSPX, Bishop Charrière comes across as much more cautious. This decree is translated by one source sympathetic to the SSPX as follows:

1. The "International Priestly Society of St. Pius X" is erected in our diocese as a *pia unio* (pious union).
2. The seat of the society is fixed as the Maison St. Pie X (St. Pius X House), 50, rue de la Vignettaz, in our episcopal city of Fribourg.
3. We approve and confirm the statutes, here joined, of the society for a period of six years *ad experimentum*, which will be able to be renewed for a similar period by tacit approval; after which, the society can be erected definitely in our diocese by the competent Roman congregation.[13]

Beginning with the second article of this decree, its intention is fairly self-explanatory. Bishop Charrière established the SSPX's headquarters at a fixed address within the territorial boundaries of his diocese. This seems to be simple enough.

Similarly, most of the third article within this decree is easily understood. Establishing the SSPX *ad experimentum* for a period of six years simply means that the SSPX was being established on an experimental basis for the next six years. Canonical establishment on an experimental basis is quite common where a diocesan bishop has certain hesitations or reservations. In the normal course of events, an institute's renewal at the end of the experimental period would have been tacitly approved for a similar period of time. The institute would then seek permission from the competent curial congregation to be definitely, that is permanently, erected in the particular diocese in which the institute was located. Thus Bishop Charrière's canonical precautions in establishing the SSPX on an experimental basis for six years are clear as to both their intent and purpose.

Nevertheless, a canonical ambiguity remains in the third article as to Bishop Charrière's intention in establishing the SSPX. The decree states: "We approve and confirm the statutes, here joined, of the society …" In looking at the first article, Bishop Charrière is obviously referring to the SSPX, which he erects as a pious union. Yet the SSPX's statutes specifically state that the SSPX is to be founded as a priestly society "of common life without vows,"[14] in accordance with Canons 673–674, and 488, Nos. 3 and 4 of the 1917 *Code of Canon Law*. Thus, a canonical ambiguity exists within the decree establishing the SSPX which will lead to some controversy during the subsequent canonical suppression of the SSPX.

In fact, even the SSPX's most ardent supporters have been forced to admit this apparent ambiguity in Bishop Charrière's decree. As one such individual comments:

> The bishop's use of the expression *"pia unio"* here is a little confusing. A *"pia unio,"* as [Canons] 707–708 make clear,

is not normally a juridical person. It means a lay association. A religious "society of common life," as the approved statutes of the Society of St. Pius X specify it is, described in [Canon] 673, is really very much like a religious institute but without public vows. It is possible that Bishop Charrière intended here "*pia domus*" since it is quite normal to erect a "*pia domus*" as the first step towards a new religious institute.[15]

To briefly explain this controversy, the SSPX claim that according to their constitutions they were erected in accordance with the norms of Canon 673 under the 1917 *Code of Canon Law*. The Latin text uses the word *societas* to describe "a society of men or women who lead a community life after the manner of religious under the government of superiors and according to approved constitutions, but without the three usual vows of religious life."[16] Such a society would differ from a pious union (*pia unio*), the word used by Bishop Charrière in his decree establishing the SSPX. Therefore, it would appear that Bishop Charrière actually established the SSPX in accordance with the definition of a pious union of the faithful provided by Canon 707, Par. 1, of the 1917 *Code of Canon Law*. Fr. Charles Augustine loosely translates this canon as follows: "Associations of the faithful founded to further some piety or charity are known as pious organizations; if they enjoy a quasi-corporate status, they are called brotherhoods (*sodalitia*)."[17]

Although several difficulties would arise between the SSPX and competent Church authorities over the interpretation of Bishop Charrière's decree, the two most serious involved the SSPX's juridical status and which hierarchical authority was competent to suppress the SSPX. With regard to juridical status, as Woywod notes in his commentary on Canon 708 from the 1917 *Code of Canon Law*, "for the erection of pious unions, the approval of the ordinary suffices ... though they are not legal persons."[18] Hence, even though the approval of the diocesan bishop was required to formally erect the SSPX, as a pious union it would not be considered a juridical person within the Catholic Church. Cutting through the canonical jargon, this would mean that a diocesan bishop would be competent to canonically suppress the SSPX without having to go to the Holy See.

This apparent ambiguity arising from the decree erecting the SSPX would be further compounded in a letter to Archbishop Lefebvre from Cardinal Wright, Prefect of the Sacred Congregation for the Clergy. Cardinal Wright congratulated Archbishop Lefebvre on the founding of his new *Associatio* (association), taking pains only to refer to the SSPX as a *Fraternitae Sacerdotalis* (priestly fraternity) in brackets.[19] And thus in utilizing the word "association" which is more in keeping with Canon 707, it would appear that Cardinal Wright recognized the canonical erection of the SSPX as merely that of a pious association of the faithful.

The Canonical Suppression of the SSPX

Like the years immediately following any Ecumenical Council within the Church's history, the period after the Second Vatican Council would prove tumultuous within the Church. Many priests gave up the priesthood, and many religious surrendered the habit. Yet the SSPX and their seminary continued to draw both vocations and international attention. Unfortunately, this attention was not always positive and eventually would lead to both the suppression of the SSPX and suspension *a divinis*[20] of Archbishop Lefebvre.

In the following passage, Archbishop Lefebvre documents the growth of the SSPX during the years immediately following its founding. He also shares his interpretation concerning the subsequent problems that arose between the Vatican and the SSPX:

> From year to year the number of seminarians increased; in 1970 there were eleven entrants and in 1974, forty. The innovators became increasingly worried. It was obvious that if we were training seminarians it was to ordain them, and that the future priests would be faithful to the Mass of the Church, the Mass of Tradition, the Mass of all time.[21]

Part of the sentiment expressed by Archbishop Lefebvre was also shared by many of his former followers who have subsequently reconciled with the Church. As Fr. Daniel Oppenheimer, one such former SSPX seminarian, notes within his licentiate thesis:

> By 1976, [Lefebvre's] society had come under open attack, particularly by certain members of the French episcopacy. Central to the complaint was the continued use of the old Roman Liturgy in his canonically approved seminary now located at Ecône, Switzerland. That this same seminary was bulging at the seams with clean-cut young Frenchmen wearing cassocks, when the seminaries in France were depleted of all but a few seminarians now sporting blue jeans and long hair in the anti-clerical mode of the day, did not help the widening gulf between the two sides.[22]

That an acrimonious situation arose during this time between the SSPX and the rest of the Church is substantiated by subsequent events. Yet even Cardinal Ratzinger partially attributes this stand-off to the great turmoil disrupting many

of the more established seminaries at the time. In his following reflection upon what led many priests and seminarians to
follow Archbishop Lefebvre, Cardinal Ratzinger states:

> Others still would like to collaborate fully in the normal pas-
> toral activity of the Church. Nevertheless, they have let them-
> selves be driven to their choice by the unsatisfactory situation
> that has arisen in the seminaries in many countries.[23]

In response to this growing tension between Archbishop
Lefebvre and various European bishops, Pope Paul VI con-
voked a commission of cardinals to examine the situation with
Archbishop Lefebvre and his SSPX seminary. The commission
arranged an apostolic visitation to the SSPX seminary for
November of 1974.

The apostolic visitation went as planned until Archbishop
Lefebvre overheard a comment expressed by one of the apostolic visitors. The archbishop began to question the orthodoxy
of this apostolic visitor, and subsequently wrote a public declaration that has since become famous in many traditionalist
circles. This declaration proved problematical to the Holy See.
In particular, the Holy See objected to the declaration's second
and third paragraphs in which the archbishop challenged the
authenticity of both the current papacy and the Second Vatican Council:

> Because of this adherence [to Eternal Rome], we refuse and
> have always refused to follow the Rome of neo-Modernist
> and neo-Protestant tendencies such as were clearly mani-
> fested during the Second Vatican Council, and after the
> Council in all the resulting reforms.

All these reforms have indeed contributed and still con-
tribute to the demolition of the Church, to the ruin of the
priesthood, to the destruction of the holy Sacrifice of the
Mass and the sacraments, to the disappearance of the religious life, and to naturalistic and Teilhardian teaching in
universities, seminaries, and catechesis, a teaching born of
liberalism and Protestantism many times condemned by the
solemn magisterium of the Church. No authority, even the
very highest in the hierarchy, can constrain us to abandon
or diminish our Catholic Faith such as it has been clearly
expressed and professed by the Church's magisterium for
nineteen centuries.[24]

To preserve the Liturgy and the spiritual discipline of the
pre-Vatican II era was one thing. However, to impugn in the
name of the pre-conciliar magisterium the validity of the post-
conciliar reforms, while questioning the authority of the post-
conciliar Church hierarchy, was another issue entirely. This
could only bring about negative canonical repercussions upon
both Archbishop Lefebvre and the SSPX. In light of Archbishop Lefebvre's public declaration and the growing threat it
posed to the good order of the local Church, Bishop Mamie,
having succeeded Bishop Charrière as bishop of Lausanne,
Geneva, and Fribourg, was forced to take disciplinary action
against Archbishop Lefebvre and the SSPX.

On January 24, 1975, Bishop Mamie wrote to the Sacred
Congregation for Religious. "Having made a careful study of
Msgr. Lefebvre's declaration," one commentator writes, "he
considered it a sad but urgent necessity to withdraw the
approval given by his predecessor to the Society of St. Pius
X."[25] Bishop Mamie received a reply dated the following April
25th in which Cardinal Tabera, the Prefect for the Sacred Con-

gregation for Religious, urged Bishop Mamie to withdraw his canonical approval from the SSPX immediately. On May 6, 1975, Bishop Mamie informed Archbishop Lefebvre "that after long months of prayer and reflection he had reached the sad but necessary decision that he must withdraw all the acts and concessions granted by his predecessor to the Society of St. Pius X."[26]

This is where the controversy over the SSPX's canonical status began to flare. With regard to the canonical suppression of a pious union or association of the faithful, for a serious reason Canon 699 of the 1917 *Code of Canon Law* permits the local ordinary to "suppress not only those associations which were erected by himself or his predecessors, but also associations erected with the consent of the local ordinary by religious in virtue of an apostolic indult."[27] Therefore, even without consulting and obtaining approval from the Sacred Congregation for Religious, as the local ordinary of the diocese in which the SSPX was erected, Bishop Mamie acted well within his canonical capacity in suppressing the SSPX.

Yet Archbishop Lefebvre maintained that the SSPX was canonically erected as a society of clerics without public vows, rather than as a pious association of the faithful. On this basis, he called into question the validity of Bishop Mamie's canonical suppression of the SSPX. Quoting canon law in one of his early works which was popular among his followers, Archbishop Lefebvre argued, "if a succeeding bishop wishes to suppress an association or fraternity, he cannot do so without recourse to Rome."[28] In other words, if the SSPX were erected as a society of clerics, Bishop Mamie could only suppress it after having received permission from the Holy See.

Lefebvre's argument would be in accord with Canon 493 of the 1917 *Code of Canon Law*. As Father Woywod explains in his following commentary on this Canon: "Any religious organization, even a diocesan congregation, which has been legally established cannot be dissolved, though it should consist of but one house, except by the Holy See ..."[29] Thus Lefebvre continued to argue that the canonical suppression of the SSPX was invalid, claiming it came from the local ordinary rather than the Holy See. Additionally, he maintained, even after the SSPX's canonical suppression, that the SSPX "is consequently recognized by Rome in a perfectly legal manner."[30]

To all outside of the SSPX, however, this argument would prove moot. For on the same day that Bishop Mamie suppressed the SSPX, Archbishop Lefebvre received a decision from the commission of cardinals convoked by Pope Paul VI to investigate both Lefebvre and the SSPX. Composed of Cardinal Garrone, Prefect of the Sacred Congregation for Catholic Education, as well as the aforementioned Cardinals Wright and Tabera, who acted on behalf of their respective congregations, the commission was troubled by Lefebvre's controversial November declaration. In fact, the commission had previously met with Archbishop Lefebvre in an unsuccessful attempt to convince the archbishop to retract his declaration.

Within the text of their decision, the commission drew the following conclusions and outlined a course of action:

> Now such a Declaration appears unacceptable to us on all points. It is impossible to reconcile most of the affirmations contained in the document with authentic fidelity to the Church, to the one who is responsible for Her, and to the Council in which the mind and will of the Church were expressed. It is inadmissible that every individual should be invited to submit papal directives to his own private judgment and decide for himself whether to accept or reject them ...

It is with the entire approval of His Holiness [Paul VI] that we communicate the following decisions to you:

1) "A letter will be dispatched to Msgr. Mamie according him the right to withdraw the approval which his predecessor gave to the fraternity and to its statutes." This has been done in a letter from His Excellency Cardinal Tabera, Prefect of the Congregation for Religious.

2) Once it is suppressed, "the society no longer having a juridical basis, its foundations, and notably the seminary at Ecône, lose by the same act the right to existence."

3) It is obvious — we are invited to notify it clearly — "that no support whatsoever can be given to Msgr. Lefebvre as long as the ideas contained in the Manifesto of 21 November continue to be the basis for his work."[31]

From the above decision of the commission of cardinals, it is clear that the Holy See was concerned with Archbishop Lefebvre's public declaration of his refusal to submit to the reforms of the Second Vatican Council and the various disciplinary reforms brought about by Pope Paul VI. Thus, certain disciplinary measures were necessary in order to correct the situation. Regardless of whether the SSPX had been erected as a pious union of the faithful or as a society of common life without public vows, the commission of cardinals had delegated Bishop Mamie the right to withdraw canonical approval from the SSPX and its statutes — a canonical right which Bishop Mamie would already possess by virtue of the law itself if, as the decree of canonical erection states, the SSPX had merely been established as a pious union of the faithful.

However, in light of Archbishop Lefebvre's argument that the SSPX was canonically erected as a society of common life without vows, and thus could only be suppressed by the Holy See, the Holy See clearly delegated this canonical right to Bishop Mamie. Moreover, as the SSPX was only erected *ad experimentum* for a period of six years, the SSPX's canonical erection was in no way permanent, and therefore even if the delegation of the right of suppression to Bishop Mamie had been invalid, Archbishop Lefebvre still could not reasonably presume either the Holy See's or the local ordinary's tacit approval beyond the completion of the six-year period. Therefore, one cannot but conclude that the SSPX, regardless of their initial juridical status, were validly suppressed in accordance with canon law.

Similarly, the commission also suppressed the seminary of the SSPX. This is an interesting fact in itself, because while the initial decree of erection approved a "seat of the society"[32] at a fixed address, it has never been clear from any of the documents presented by the SSPX that their seminary had been canonically erected. However, given the apostolic visitation to the seminary which preceded Archbishop Lefebvre's declaration, and given the commission's decision explicitly stating that the seminary is to be suppressed, the present author will concede the possibility that the SSPX seminary had been erected in accordance with canon law. Nevertheless, upon suppression of the SSPX, the commission decreed that the SSPX no longer had any juridical basis, and, hence its foundation and seminary were also thereby extinguished. Therefore, Bishop Mamie was delegated the authority to suppress not only the SSPX, but its various foundations as well, including the seminary.

Nevertheless, Archbishop Lefebvre could question whether the decision was an act of the commission or whether "the entire approval of His Holiness" noted in the decision meant that it had been rendered *in forma specifica*. As a result, in a letter to Cardinal Staffa and the Supreme Tribunal of the Apostolic Signatura, Archbishop Lefebvre attempted recourse against the decision of the commission of cardinals with the following statement:

> Against the form in which the decisions were taken expressed in the letter of May 6, 1975, as well by His Excellency Msgr. Mamie, bishop of Fribourg, as by the three cardinals who signed the letter addressed to me from Rome ... This form of procedure is contrary to Canon 493 of the *Codex Juris Canonici*.
>
> Against the competence of the commission of cardinals which condemns me on a matter of faith because of my declaration which appeared in the review *Itinéraires* and which I wrote on November 21, 1974. I demand to be judged by the only tribunal competent in these matters, the Sacred Congregation for the Doctrine of the Faith.
>
> Against the sentence pronounced by Msgr. Mamie and approved by the cardinals of the commission; in fact, my declaration, if it deserves condemnation, should condemn me personally and not destroy my fraternity, nor the seminary, nor the houses that have been erected ...[33]

As is visible from the content of Archbishop Lefebvre's appeal, he accepted neither the decision of the commission of cardinals nor the actions of Bishop Mamie in suppressing the SSPX. His argument to the Apostolic Signatura was based upon three grounds: that proper procedure was not followed in suppressing the SSPX and their seminary; that the commission of cardinals was not competent to judge his declaration, rather only the Sacred Congregation for the Doctrine of the Faith was competent for this; and that the declaration was his alone, and neither the SSPX nor their seminary should be suppressed as a result of his personal declaration.

Whether or not the normal canonical procedure had been meticulously followed would soon become irrelevant. On June 10, 1975, the Apostolic Signatura, which is the Church's supreme court, rejected Archbishop Lefebvre's appeal on the grounds that the Holy Father had approved the decision of the commission of cardinals *in forma specifica*.[34] The phrase "*in forma specifica*" means that the Holy Father made his own the decision of the commission of cardinals. Pope Paul VI confirmed this to be the case in a personal letter he wrote to Archbishop Lefebvre. In it, the Holy Father stated: "Finally, the conclusions which [the commission of cardinals] proposed to us, we made all and each of them ours, and we personally ordered that they be immediately put into force."[35]

In canonical terms, this meant that no further recourse was available to Archbishop Lefebvre against the canonical suppression of the SSPX. For under Canon 1880 of the 1917 *Code of Canon Law*, "there is no appeal: (1) from the sentence of the Supreme Pontiff himself or from the *Signatura Apostolica* ..."[36] Consequently, the SSPX and their seminary were unquestionably suppressed as a juridical person within the Church.

CHAPTER THREE

Archbishop Lefebvre's Unlawful Ordination of Seminarians

"*To punish me for my contempt for authority, fate made me an authority myself.*"

— ALBERT EINSTEIN

Questioning the Pope

During the following year, Archbishop Lefebvre simply ignored the canonical suppression of both the SSPX and its seminary. Instead, he chose to believe that Pope Paul VI was being mismanaged by his curia, and thus was not really aware of what was taking place in the broader context of the Church. Such a mindset only foreshadowed future controversy between the archbishop and the Vatican. As Fr. Hans Urs von Balthasar notes in his modern defense of the Petrine Papacy, "in most instances, complaints do not begin with charges against the Pope's person but against his retinue: it is the cardinals, the curia who are all at fault. Ever since the curia was established, complaints have not ceased."[37] Archbishop Lefebvre shared such a mindset. Thus additional problems with the Church hierarchy became inevitable.

As the summer of 1976 approached, Archbishop Lefebvre's initial class of SSPX seminarians found themselves on the verge of graduation. Their ordination became a touchy issue given the canonical suppression of the SSPX during the previous year. With little hesitation, Archbishop Lefebvre announced his intention to ordain his seminarians and incardinate them into the SSPX. Lefebvre and his followers argued that "despite the letter from Pope Paul dated June 29, 1975, the entire legal process taken against the [SSPX] had been so irregular that it could not be considered as having been legally suppressed."[38]

A short aside to explain the issue of incardination is in order. Historically, no cleric within the Catholic Church can be headless. (The Church may occasionally tolerate *mindless* clergy, but never a headless one.) Thus, every priest and deacon is subject either to a bishop or a major religious superior, and every bishop must be tied to a diocese — either actual, as in the case of a diocesan bishop, or titular, as in the case of an auxiliary bishop. Therefore, a bishop or major religious superior serves as the head of every priest and deacon, and the Bishop of Rome serves as the head of every bishop and every superior general.

To prevent her clergy from wandering about without the benefit of immediate oversight, the Church historically requires that her clergy be incardinated into a specific diocese or institute of consecrated life. Thus incardination is basically a means of registration particular to the priesthood. No cleric is permitted to minister to the faithful without the benefit of incardination.

Against Lefebvre's intention, substituting on behalf of the Vatican Secretariat of State, Msgr. Benelli sent Msgr. Amborio Marchioni, the Papal Nuncio at Berne, the following instruction: "You should, at the same time, inform Msgr. Marcel

Lefebvre that, *de mandato speciali Summa Pontificis*, in the present circumstances and according to the presciptions of [Canon] 2373, 1, of the [1917] *Code of Canon Law*, he must strictly abstain from conferring orders from the moment he receives the present injunction."[39]

Under the 1917 *Code of Canon Law*, Canon 955 required every candidate for ordination to the diaconate or priesthood to be ordained "by his own proper bishop or with legitimate dimissorial letters received from him."[40] A dimissorial letter is simply a letter from the candidate's bishop or major superior giving permission to another bishop to ordain the candidate. The first paragraph of Canon 2373 of the same code "legislates that those who ordain the subject of another ordinary in violation of the precept of Canon 955, are automatically suspended *ab ordinum collatione*, or 'from the conferring of orders for one year reserved to the Apostolic See.'"[41]

The suspension is reserved to the Apostolic See, meaning only the Holy See may judge the situation and enforce the automatic penalty. If the Holy See judges a bishop as having violated Canon 955 with just cause or through a legitimate misunderstanding, then he can lift the suspension against the bishop in question. Part of the intention here is to allow both a bishop and the Holy See canonical equity in certain exceptional situations that are unforeseen by the Holy Father in legislating this canon.

Nevertheless, Archbishop Lefebvre received his warning *de mandato speciali Summa Pontificis* (by means of special mandate from the Supreme Pontiff). Hence, Lefebvre could reasonably presume that the Apostolic See foresaw his situation. Obviously, the Holy Father did not consider the circumstances in which the archbishop found himself as sufficient cause to violate Canon 955. Therefore, if Archbishop Lefebvre personally proceeded with the ordination of his seminarians, in accordance with the first paragraph of Canon 2373 of the 1917 *Code of Canon Law,* "he would automatically be suspended from conferring orders for a period of one year."

Whether or not Lefebvre subjectively believed the Pope had suppressed his society was now irrelevant in light of the objective juridical facts. Archbishop Lefebvre knew that the will of the Roman Pontiff forbade him from proceeding with the ordinations. Therefore, he knew how the highest authority in the Church would interpret the law as it applied to his situation.

Yet in response to the canonical warning he had received, Archbishop Lefebvre wrote the following in a public letter addressed to the Holy Father: "Will Your Holiness please fully understand the sorrow which grips me, and my stupefaction, on the one side at hearing the paternal appeals Your Holiness addresses to me, and on the other the cruelty of the blows which do not cease striking us, the latest of them striking worst of all my dear seminarians and their families on the eve of their priesthood for which they have been preparing for five or six years."[42]

While Archbishop Lefebvre found this prohibition harsh — especially given the canonical warning's proximity to the date scheduled for the ordination of his seminarians — the fact remains that Rome had suppressed the SSPX and its seminary approximately a year before. Therefore, Rome's actions were hardly surprising, and ought to have been anticipated by Lefebvre and his followers.

In revisiting this incident, some of Lefebvre's apologists argue the archbishop had an obligation in justice to ordain his seminarians to the priesthood. Yet Canon 970 of the 1917 *Code of Canon Law* permits the proper bishop or the competent major religious superior to deny his seminarians ordination to the diaconate or priesthood for any canonical reason, even one that is not public knowledge, without canonical procedure. Additionally, while some might leave the determination whether or not to proceed with any ordinations up to Archbishop Lefebvre, there are several canonical issues that prevented Lefebvre from lawfully acting in such a capacity.

First, as previously noted, the SSPX had not been founded as a religious order but a pious association of the faithful. A pious association of the faithful enjoys no juridical personality under the 1917 *Code of Canon Law*, meaning its members are subject to the diocesan bishop. In short, a candidate for major orders must incardinate either into a diocese or into an institute of consecrated life (i.e. the Franciscans, a Benedictine Monastery, etc.) As merely a pious union of the faithful, the SSPX would not qualify for the latter.

Second, even if the SSPX had at one time enjoyed juridical personality, the SSPX remained, according to their statutes, an *ad experimentum* society without common vows and of diocesan right. This means the SSPX was initially established on an experimental basis and subject to the oversight of the diocesan bishop. Upon receiving major orders — that is, ordination to the diaconate or priesthood — its clerics would incardinate into a diocese rather than into the SSPX. Thus the competent authority with regard to ordination and incardination remained the diocesan bishop. As the Vatican Secretariat of State clearly pointed out to Archbishop Lefebvre, the SSPX seminarians were not Lefebvre's subjects in this matter, but those of another ordinary.

Third, as previously mentioned, Rome had canonically suppressed the SSPX and their seminary. Therefore, the SSPX could no longer claim any juridical status. This canonical suppression had taken place, *in forma specifica*, approximately a

year before the scheduled ordinations which led to Archbishop
Lefebvre's suspension *ab ordinum collatione*. That Lefebvre and
his seminarians chose to ignore these canonical suppressions of
their pious union and its seminary was their prerogative; nevertheless, in so doing they forfeited any canonical right to
expect ordination from the Church. The Church could not
assume that the SSPX's seminarians met the canonical quali-
fications necessary for the lawful reception of ordination to
the diaconate and priesthood.

Finally, ignoring the hard facts for a moment, let us suppose Archbishop Lefebvre was legitimately the major superior
of an existing institute with juridical personality. Let us also
suppose that a priest or deacon was canonically capable of
incardinating into this institute. In accordance with Canon
218 of the 1917 *Code of Canon Law*, by divine positive law the
Roman Pontiff retains ordinary supreme power and universal
jurisdiction over the discipline and government of the Church.
As Woywod explains in his commentary on this canon, "This
power is episcopal, ordinary and immediate, and extends over
each and every church, and over each and every pastor as well
as over the faithful, and is independent of all human authority."[43] Therefore, even under such a fictional scenario in which
the archbishop is the major superior of an established institute,
the authority of Pope Paul VI as the Roman Pontiff supercedes
that of Archbishop Lefebvre as major superior. Such is the
nature of the Roman Pontiff's supreme and universal jurisdiction.

Nevertheless, as Woywod explains in his commentary on
Canon 970, a cleric who has been prohibited by his ordinary
from receiving major orders would normally have the right of
recourse to the Holy See.[44] However, recourse would be
improbable in the case of the SSPX as the instruction pro-

hibiting Lefebvre from ordaining his seminarians had initially come from the Holy See, by special mandate of the Supreme Pontiff. The mind of the Holy Father was confirmed in a second letter from the Secretariat of State, in which Msgr. Benelli directly responds to Archbishop Lefebvre's aforementioned letter to Pope Paul VI.

In his response on behalf of the Holy Father, Msgr. Benelli states:

> The Holy Father has received your letter of 22 June. He desires me to inform you of his mind on this subject ... The Holy Father charges me this very day to confirm the measure of which you have been informed in his name, *de mandato speciali*: You are to abstain, now, from conferring any [holy] order. Do not use as a pretext the confused state of the seminarians who were to be ordained; this is just the opportunity to explain to them and to their families that you cannot ordain them to the service of the Church against the will of the supreme Pastor of the Church. There is nothing desperate in their case; if they have good will and are seriously prepared for a presbyteral ministry in genuine fidelity to the conciliar Church ... Those responsible will find the best solution for them, but they must begin with an act of obedience to the Church.[45]

Msgr. Benelli concluded his letter by repeating the canonical penalties both Archbishop Lefebvre and his candidates would incur if Lefebvre proceeded with his intended ordinations. Nevertheless, what is extremely clear is that the mind of the supreme legislator had been clearly stated to Lefebvre and his seminarians. In light of Canon 17 of the 1917 *Code of Canon Law*, which states that laws are authoritatively interpreted by the legislator and his successors, it is important to keep in mind that while Lefebvre's interpretation of the canons differed from that of the Holy Father, the latter is the supreme legislator within the Church. This means that the Bishop of Rome may promulgate laws that bind the whole Church. Similarly, Canon 17 establishes that how the Holy Father interprets the law also binds the whole Church, if such is the Holy Father's intention. Thus, as universal legislator, the Roman Pontiff's interpretation not only prevails, but it has the same force as the law itself.[46]

In the case of the second warning to Lefebvre, as with the first one, Msgr. Benelli issued it not upon his personal authority as substitute of the Secretary of State, but *de mandato speciali* Pope Paul VI. Hence, Archbishop Lefebvre's warning had come from the special mandate of Pope Paul VI himself. In short, Lefebvre's canonical obligation at this point in time was not to interpret canon law to his own end, but to submit in obedience to the will of the Roman Pontiff.

Archbishop Lefebvre Is Suspended from Performing Future Ordinations

Yet despite his canonical obligation, on June 29th, 1976, Archbishop Lefebvre obstinately chose to proceed with the ordination of his seminarians to the priesthood. During his homily at the ordination, the archbishop attempted the following justification of his disobedience to the Holy Father: "I myself shall probably be struck by suspension. These young priests will be struck [with] an irregularity which in theory should prevent them from saying Holy Mass. It is possible. Well, I appeal to St. Pius V — St. Pius V, who in his bull[47] said that, in perpetuity, no priest could incur a censure, whatever it might be, in perpetuity, for saying this [Tridentine] Mass. And consequently, this censure, this excommunication, if there was one, these censures, are absolutely invalid, contrary to that which St. Pius V established in perpetuity in his bull: that *never in any age could one inflict a censure on a priest who says this Mass.*"[48]

Without straying too far into the liturgical debate between Archbishop Lefebvre and Pope Paul VI, the following two fallacies immediately become apparent in Lefebvre's justification of his act of disobedience. First, in appealing to the papal authority of St. Pius V and *Quo Primum Tempore*, Lefebvre again neglects Canon 17 of the 1917 *Code of Canon Law*. For although Pius V promulgated *Quo Primum Tempore* as supreme legislator, the authority to interpret the legislative and disciplinary elements of this papal bull rested with Pope Paul VI, who is Pius V's lawful successor as universal legislator, and not Archbishop Lefebvre. Therefore, Lefebvre's appeal to the legislative authority of Pius V to justify his act of disobedience to Paul VI cannot be canonically sustained in light of Canon 17.

As a canonical aside to this argument, St. Pius V could not bind Pope Paul VI to the dictates of *Quo Primum Tempore*. For this papal bull is a matter of ecclesiastical discipline, and as such is always subject to change depending upon the current needs of the Church. These needs may evolve or change over time, or else a future Roman Pontiff may understand and interpret these needs differently. Thus the old Roman adage, which the Church has adopted as a canonical principle, that "equals have no power over one another."

Yet the whole debate over whether *Quo Primum Tempore* was perpetual or whether it had been abrogated is secondary to this controversy. For the Holy See never directly threatened

Archbishop Lefebvre with suspension *ab ordinum collatione* for celebrating Mass according to the Tridentine missal, but for ordaining seminarians to major orders without dimmissorial letters from their proper ordinary.

Moreover, Lefebvre was doing so against the express will of the Roman Pontiff, who in light of Canon 218 of the 1917 *Code of Canon Law* retains universal ordinary power. Therefore, even supposing *Quo Primum Tempore* gave Lefebvre canonical permission to continue celebrating Mass according the pre-Vatican II liturgical usage, *Quo Primum Tempore* does not authorize a bishop to unlawfully ordain seminarians to the priesthood or the diaconate — particularly when such ordinations are contrary to the expressed will of the Roman Pontiff. Not even the intention to provide priests for the celebration of the Tridentine Mass could trump such a direct command. Thus the various arguments put forward by Lefebvre and his followers based upon *Quo Primum Tempore* are not canonically applicable to the situation in which Lefebvre and his seminarians found themselves.

In light of Lefebvre's act of disobedience, Fr. Romeo Panciroli, acting as spokesman for the Press Bureau of the Holy See, declared the following day that: "Msgr. Lefebvre has automatically incurred suspension for a year from the conferring of orders, a suspension reserved to the Apostolic See."[49] In addition, the Holy See announced that censures would be imposed upon those seminarians who unlawfully received ordination from Lefebvre, stating that "those who have been ordained are *ipso facto* suspended from the order received, and, if they were exercise it, they would be in an irregular and criminal situation."[50] Cardinal Baggio subsequently confirmed these suspensions on behalf of the Sacred Congregation for Bishops.[51]

Archbishop Lefebvre's Suspension from All Priestly Faculties

After his illicit ordination of seminarians to major orders, the censures imposed upon Archbishop Lefebvre would not end with suspension *ab ordinum collatione.* For at the same press conference, Father Panciroli also announced the following: "The Holy See is examining the special case of formal disobedience of Msgr. Lefebvre to the instructions of the Holy Father who, by the documents of June 12 and 25, 1976, expressly forbade him to proceed with the ordinations."[52]

In announcing the examination of a case of formal disobedience against Archbishop Lefebvre, the Holy See made it obvious that he was concerned about the direction Lefebvre was leading the SSPX. In less than a week after being suspended *ab ordinum collatione,* Lefebvre received a formal canonical warning from Cardinal Baggio, the Prefect of the Sacred Congregation of Bishops. After restating the actions which led to Lefebvre's suspension *ab ordinum collatione,* Cardinal Baggio states as follows:

> If, however, the invitation [to repair the scandal caused by the illicit ordinations] were to prove vain, and if a proof of recognition of error did not arrive at this Congregation within ten days of your receipt of my letter, you must know that, basing itself on a special mandate of the Sovereign Pontiff, it will be the duty of this Congregation to proceed against you by inflicting the necessary penalties, in conformity with Canon 2331, Par. 1.[53]

On July 11, 1976, Archbishop Lefebvre received this formal canonical warning, signing "a certificate of reception as evidence of this fact."[54] In accordance with Canon 2331 of the 1917 *Code of Canon Law,* because of his act of disobedience to the Roman Pontiff, Archbishop Lefebvre was now receiving a formal canonical warning that he would have further censures imposed upon him unless he took immediate steps to repair the scandal he had caused. As Woywod explains in his commentary on this particular canon, "Persons who stubbornly refuse to obey the legitimate precepts or prohibitions of the Roman Pontiff or their proper ordinary shall be punished with appropriate penalties, not excluding censures, in proportion to the gravity of their guilt."[55]

In questioning the validity of the formal canonical warning as well as the ensuing suspension *a divinis*, Lefebvre and his followers applied many of the same canonical arguments that they had previously used — arguments which we have already refuted. Lefebvre clearly was not deterred from his course of disobedience by the threat of further censures; he had begun to solidify in his rejection of the Second Vatican Council which he believed to be destroying the Church, as noted in his following response to Paul VI regarding the formal warning:

> Let Your Holiness abandon that ill-omened undertaking of compromise with the ideas of modern man, an undertaking which originates in a secret understanding between high dignitaries in the Church and those of Masonic lodges since before the Council … To persevere in that direction is to pursue the destruction of the Church. Your Holiness will easily understand that we cannot collaborate in so calamitous a purpose, which we should do were we to close our seminaries.[56]

Needless to say, this was neither the retraction nor the act of obedience from Lefebvre that the Holy See had hoped for as a result of the canonical warning. At best, Archbishop Lefebvre now accused Pope Paul VI of unintentionally collaborating with freemasonry in order to destroy the Church. It was also evident that Lefebvre would not submit to the authority of the Roman Pontiff. In light of Lefebvre's obstinacy, the Sacred Congregation for Bishops further imposed the sanction of suspension *a divinis* — in other words, a suspension from all priestly faculties — upon Lefebvre on July 22, 1976, within the following notification:

> The Holy Father has informed me that he has received from you a letter dated 17 July. In his eyes, it unhappily could not be considered satisfactory — on the contrary. I may even tell you that he is very distressed by the attitude to him shown in that document ... In consequence, the Sovereign Pontiff Paul VI, on July 22, 1976, in conformity with Canon 2227, in virtue of which the penalties that can be applied to a bishop are expressly reserved to him, has inflicted on you suspension *a divinis* provided for in Canon 2279, 2, 2E, and has ordered that it take immediate effect.[57]

Having found both Lefebvre's behavior and his refusal to repair the scandal he had caused unacceptable, the Holy Father suspended Lefebvre *a divinis* according to the norms of Canons 2227 and 2279 of the 1917 *Code of Canon Law*. As Woywod explains, "Suspension *a divinis* forbids the exercise of every act of the power of orders which one obtained either by sacred orders or by privilege."[58] Thus Lefebvre was now forbidden by the Holy See from the exercise of holy orders, a prohibition reserved to the Holy Father personally. In other words, his suspension was now perpetual until its absolution by the Holy Father, and applicable to more than simply the ordination of seminarians to the diaconate and priesthood.

CHAPTER FOUR

The Schism and Excommunication of Archbishop Lefebvre

"WHAT A LONG, strange trip it's been."

— THE GRATEFUL DEAD

From Protocol Agreement to Excommunication

While some correspondence between Archbishop Lefebvre and the Holy See continued in the years after his suspension *a divinis*, there would be little notable canonical development until May 5, 1988, when Archbishop Lefebvre and Cardinal Ratzinger signed a protocol agreement regularizing the situation of the SSPX. Unfortunately, less than two months after signing the protocol agreement, Lefebvre would retract his signature and proceed to consecrate bishops against the express mandate of the Roman Pontiff. The Holy See responded by declaring Lefebvre excommunicated, resulting in the present schism between Rome and the SSPX.

After intense negotiation, on May 5, 1988, Archbishop Lefebvre and Cardinal Ratzinger signed a protocol agreement between the Holy See and the SSPX. The protocol regularized the SSPX as a clerical society of apostolic life of pontifical right, which bestowed upon the SSPX a status similar to that of a religious order responsible directly to the Holy Father.

The protocol agreement also lifted all suspensions against the clergy affiliated with the SSPX, while regularizing the status of any SSPX adherents among the laity. Most importantly, the protocol agreement provided for the future pastoral care of any clergy and laity associated with the SSPX. For his part, Archbishop Lefebvre recognized the authenticity of the Second Vatican Council and the reformed Roman Liturgy of Paul VI.

The protocol agreement also laid the practical groundwork for the future of the traditionalist movement. Besides regularizing chapels affiliated with the SSPX — chapels which, up until this point, were neither recognized by Rome nor by local diocesan bishops — the Holy See granted the SSPX permission to continue using the liturgical missal of 1962. Having obtained the approval of the Holy Father, Cardinal Ratzinger also promised the SSPX a candidate from among the ranks of the SSPX priests whom Archbishop Lefebvre would be permitted to consecrate to the episcopacy.

The English translation of this particular text within the protocol agreement is as follows:

> 5.2. But, for practical and psychological reasons, the consecration of a member of the [SSPX] as a bishop seems useful. This is why, in the context of the doctrinal and canonical solution of reconciliation, we suggest to the Holy Father that he name a bishop chosen from among the members of the [SSPX], presented by Archbishop Lefebvre. In consequence of the principle indicated above (5.1.), this bishop as a rule

is not the superior general of the society. But it seems opportune that he be a member of the Roman commission.

In short, the new bishop would provide for the ordination of SSPX clergy and the confirmation of tridentinist laity according to the 1962 liturgical usage. Additionally, the Holy See agreed to establish a Roman commission composed of members named from both the Holy See and the SSPX, of which the SSPX bishop would be a member *ex officio*. The main purpose of the Roman commission would be to resolve future questions arising between the Holy See and the SSPX.

Yet if the Holy See thought that most problems between the Church and the SSPX had been resolved, new problems began to surface almost immediately over the consecration of bishops. The Holy See had agreed to consecrate a bishop for the SSPX, fixing the date for August 15, 1988. In a letter to Cardinal Ratzinger dated May 24, 1988, Lefebvre began to waiver from the protocol agreement, stating:

> Upon reflection, it appears clear that the goal of these dialogues is to reabsorb us within the conciliar Church, the only Church to which you make allusion during these meetings ... Therefore, with much regret we feel obliged to ask that, before the date of June 1st, you indicate clearly to us what the intentions of the Holy See are on these two points: consecration of three bishops asked for June 30th and a majority of members from tradition in the Roman commission ... Without an answer to this request, I shall proceed with the publication of the names of the candidates to the episcopacy whom I will consecrate on June 30th with the collaboration of His Excellency Bishop de Castro Mayer.

In effect, three main problems arise out of Lefebvre's letter. First, it would appear that Lefebvre and the SSPX had adopted an attitude of schism, in not wishing to be part of the "[post-] conciliar Church." In light of his suspicion, Lefebvre now requested that a majority of the members on the Roman commission be named from his movement, rather than two of the five as outlined in the protocol agreement. Perhaps some arrangement would have been possible with regard to the Roman commission, but it was Lefebvre's other demand which proved more problematic for the Holy See. No longer satisfied with a single bishop to be consecrated on August 15th of the same year, Lefebvre now threatened to proceed illegally if Rome would not meet his demand of more bishops at a sooner date.

In response to Lefebvre's new demands, Cardinal Ratzinger wrote Lefebvre on May 30, 1988, clearly stating the Holy See's position as follows:

> Concerning the first point, the Holy Father deems it proper to adhere to the principles fixed in point II/2 of the protocol which you accepted. This commission is an organism of the Holy See in the service of the [SSPX] and the diverse instances which will have to be handled to establish and consolidate the work of reconciliation. Moreover, it is not the commission, but the Holy Father who in the final analysis will make the decisions; thus the question of a majority does not arise; the interests of the society are guaranteed by its representation within the commission, and the fears which you have expressed are groundless, since the choice of members will be made by the Holy Father himself ... Regarding the second point, the Holy Father confirms what I had already indicated to you on his behalf, namely that he is disposed to appoint a member of the [SSPX] as a bishop (in the sense of point

II/5.2. of the protocol), and to accelerate the usual process of nomination, so that the consecration could take place on the closing of the Marian year, this coming August 15.

Essentially, Cardinal Ratzinger outlined the position of the Holy See as to what was agreed upon with regard to the Roman commission and the consecration of bishops. On the topic of the Roman commission, Cardinal Ratzinger called upon Archbishop Lefebvre to honor his signature, firmly reminding him that his rights would be safeguarded by the representation of the SSPX on this commission. Nevertheless, the final authority must lay with the Roman Pontiff.

With regard to the consecration of bishops, both the Holy See and the SSPX agreed within the protocol agreement to the consecration of a single bishop, for which the Holy See had set a specific date. Hence, the position of the Holy See with regard to these issues was clearly articulated by Cardinal Ratzinger both in the protocol agreement and in his subsequent correspondence with Lefebvre.

Nevertheless, rather than bring Lefebvre into obedience and thus reconcile the SSPX with the Holy See, the negative response to Lefebvre's requests would serve as the basis for his first canonical argument in support of his illicit consecration of bishops. In a letter to the Holy Father dated June 2, 1988, Lefebvre writes:

> That is why we are asking for several bishops chosen from within the Catholic tradition, and for a majority of the members on the projected Roman commission for tradition, in order to protect ourselves against all compromise ... Given the refusal to consider our requests, and it being evident that the purpose of this reconciliation is not at all the

same in the eyes of the Holy See as it is in our eyes, we
believe it preferable to wait for times more propitious for
the return of Rome to tradition ... We shall give ourselves
the means to carry on the work which providence has
entrusted to us, being assured by His Eminence Cardinal
Ratzinger's letter of May 30th that the episcopal consecration is not contrary to the will of the Holy See, since it was
granted for August 15th.

While the above quotation from Lefebvre reveals the spirit
of schism which had begun to overtake him, a more immediate canonical issue arises, namely whether or not Lefebvre truly
had the mandate from the Holy See to proceed with the episcopal consecrations of four bishops on June 30, 1988. For as
Canon 1013 clearly states, "no bishop is permitted to consecrate anyone as bishop, unless it is first established that a pontifical mandate has been issued." With Cardinal Ratzinger's
letter of May 30, Lefebvre would maintain that he had the
necessary pontifical mandate to proceed with the episcopal
consecrations of June 30, 1988.

In light of the present canonical jurisprudence of the
Catholic Church, Lefebvre's assertion of a mandate is at best ten-
uous. While "Archbishop Lefebvre does not say here that the
Holy See agrees with all the particular circumstances of the consecrations, merely to its principle," the particulars vis-à-vis the
episcopal consecrations disputed by Lefebvre are serious enough
that they cannot be divorced from the agreement in principle
with the Holy See. For Canon 17 dictates as follows: "Ecclesiastical laws are to be understood according to the proper meaning of the words considered in their text and context. If the
meaning remains doubtful or obscure, there must be recourse

to parallel places, if there be any, to the purpose and circumstances of the law, and to the mind of the legislator."

One cannot dispute that the Holy See had accepted Cardinal Ratzinger's recommendation permitting Lefebvre be permitted to consecrate a single bishop from among the SSPX. However, the Holy See clearly intended to permit the provision of a bishop within the context of a protocol agreement which would reconcile the SSPX to the Holy See. Whereas the context within which Lefebvre now claimed the mandate to proceed with the consecration of multiple bishops is one of prolonged irregularity. Thus, both the meaning and the context of the mandate to consecrate a bishop are abundantly clear within the protocol agreement, and neither is in accord with Lefebvre's interpretation.

This raises a second problem with regard to Lefebvre's claim of a papal mandate for his episcopal consecrations: that of the mind of the Roman Pontiff with regard to the particulars in mandating for the provision of an SSPX bishop. The mind of the Holy Father, as clearly indicated within the protocol agreement, and subsequently confirmed by Cardinal Ratzinger in his letter to Lefebvre, was that Lefebvre be permitted to consecrate a single bishop to be named by the Holy See from among the members of the SSPX. The Holy See later provided a specific date for the episcopal consecration, that of August 15, 1988. Yet from this permission, Lefebvre now claimed a mandate in principle to consecrate at an earlier date multiple bishops of his choosing, which was clearly contrary to the mind of the Holy See in allowing for the provision of a single SSPX bishop. Hence, Lefebvre could not honestly claim adherence to the mandate of the Holy Father in proceeding with multiple episcopal consecrations at a date of his own choosing.

However, even if the SSPX were to argue neither the context nor the mind of the Holy Father was clear within the protocol agreement, and thus Canon 17 is inapplicable to the situation — an argument which would seem hypothetical at best given the fact that in his letters to Cardinal Ratzinger and the Holy Father, Lefebvre admits both the mind and context of the Holy See in mandating for the provision of an SSPX bishop within the protocol agreement — the obligation still exists on the part of Lefebvre not to simply interpret a broad mandate in principle from the Holy See. Rather, having sought recourse to the Holy See as to the interpretation of the clause which provides for the consecration of a bishop, Lefebvre was obliged to abide by the response given to him by Cardinal Ratzinger. For in accordance with the first paragraph of Canon 16, "Laws are authentically interpreted by the legislator and by that person to whom the legislator entrusts the power of authentic interpretation."

In effect, whatever ambiguity remained after the signing of the protocol agreement as to the interpretation of the provision for the consecration of a bishop was to be lawfully interpreted by the Holy See. Having been entrusted by Pope John Paul II with the authentic interpretation of the protocol agreement, once Cardinal Ratzinger reiterated the Holy See's position with regard to the consecration of a bishop, Lefebvre was obliged under the first paragraph of Canon 16 to adhere to this interpretation. Therefore, Lefebvre's assumption of an agreement in principle for the episcopal consecrations of his own choosing is contrary to the canonical legislation in force at the time of the protocol agreement.

In light of the above application of general norms, Lefebvre's followers simply cannot sustain their argument in favor of validly possessing a mandate in principle from the Holy See to proceed with the consecration of bishops; for in ignoring the context and intention of the legislator with which the mandate was granted, as well as in unilaterally changing the particulars of the initial mandate against the express will of the legislator, Lefebvre acted against the express mandate of the Holy See in consecrating multiple bishops.

The Excommunication

On June 9, 1988, Pope John Paul II replied to Lefebvre's letter of June 2, exhorting him not to proceed with the illicit consecration of bishops, and reiterating the position of the Holy See as follows:

> In the letter you sent me you appear to reject all that was agreed on in the previous conversations, since you clearly manifest your intention to "provide the means yourself to continue your work," particularly by proceeding shortly and without apostolic mandate to one or several episcopal ordinations, and this in flagrant contradiction not only with the norms of canon law, but also with the protocol signed on May 5th and the directions relevant to this problem contained in the letter which Cardinal Ratzinger wrote to you on my instructions on May 30th.

In the above letter Archbishop Lefebvre was clearly forewarned by the Holy Father that he lacked the necessary pontifical mandate to proceed with his episcopal consecrations, and in so doing he would violate both the norms of canon law as well as the protocol agreement. Furthermore, the Holy Father confirmed that his mind in this matter had been clearly stated by Cardinal Ratzinger in his letter of May 30th.

This did not deter Lefebvre from proceeding with his press conference on June 15, 1988, in order to publicly announce the names of the four candidates he intended to consecrate to episcopacy on June 30, 1988. In light of this announcement of the four candidates, Cardinal Gantin, on behalf of the Congregation for Bishops, issued the following official canonical warning on June 17, 1988:

> Since, on June 15th, 1988, you stated that you intended to ordain four priests to the episcopate without having obtained the mandate of the Supreme Pontiff as required by Canon 1013 of the *Code of Canon Law*, I myself convey to you this public canonical warning, confirming that if you should carry out your intention as stated above, you yourself and also the bishops ordained by you shall incur *ipso facto* excommunication *latae sententiae* reserved to the Apostolic See in accordance with Canon 1382.

The latter part of the canonical warning reiterates what is legislated in Canon 1382: that one who consecrates a bishop without a pontifical mandate, as well as those who receive such a consecration, are automatically excommunicated by the law itself, and such an excommunication can only be lifted by the Apostolic See. Lefebvre, however, was still not deterred, and on June 30, 1988, followed through with his threat and consecrated four candidates from the SSPX to the episcopacy without papal mandate. Through this act of disobedience and violation of ecclesiastical law, Lefebvre had now consummated the growing SSPX schism from Rome, automatically incurring excommunication.

Subsequently, the automatic excommunication against Lefebvre was declared by Cardinal Gantin in a decree from the Congregation for Bishops dated July 1, 1988, the day after the illicit consecrations. Acting in his official capacity on behalf of the Pope, Cardinal Gantin solemnly declares:

> Msgr. Marcel Lefebvre, Archbishop—Bishop Emeritus of Tulle, notwithstanding the formal canonical warning of 17 June last and the repeated appeals to desist from his intention, has performed a schismatic act by the episcopal consecration of four priests, without pontifical mandate and contrary to the will of the Supreme Pontiff, and has therefore incurred the penalty envisaged by Canon 1364, Par. 1, and Canon 1382 of the *Code of Canon Law* ... Having taken account of all the juridical effects, I declare that the abovementioned Archbishop Lefebvre, and Bernard Fellay, Bernard Tissier de Mallerais, Richard Williamson, and Alfonso de Galarreta have incurred *ipso facto* excommunication *latae sententiae* reserved to the Apostolic See.

As is visible from the decree of the Congregation for Bishops, having consecrated bishops without a valid pontifical mandate and against express wishes of the Holy See, Lefebvre automatically incurred excommunication reserved to the Apostolic See. Yet against this decree, Lefebvre's apologists would argue "that the above decree is not the sentence of a judge, but rather a declaration that Canons 1364 and 1382 apply." That the excommunication is *latae sententiae*, meaning it was imposed automatically by canon law, rather than *ferendae sententiae*, which is to say imposed by a judge after an ecclesiastical trial, is completely irrelevant in establishing the validity of Lefebvre's excommunication.

As Canon 331 states, "by virtue of his office, [the Roman Pontiff] has supreme, full, immediate, and universal ordinary power in the Church, and he can always freely exercise this power." In regard to Canon 1382, the Roman Pontiff has utilized his supreme legislative power to establish by law a *latae sententiae* excommunication for those who consecrate a bishop without papal mandate. In accordance with Canon 17, such an ecclesiastical law must be understood according to the mind of the legislator, and in accordance with the first paragraph of Canon 16, such a law is authentically interpreted by the legislator.

In the case of Archbishop Lefebvre, both the legislator's mind and interpretation regarding Canon 1382 were clearly and personally communicated to Lefebvre by the supreme legislator previous to Lefebvre's violation of Canon 1382. Furthermore, the very fact that Lefebvre proceeded publicly in his act of disobedience means his violation of Canon 1013 was external, and hence the third paragraph of Canon 1321 presumes his imputability in consecrating bishops without papal mandate. Therefore, neither his actions nor his imputability need be established in a judicial process.

With regard to the penalties imposed by the first paragraph of Canon 1364, this norm establishes that "a schismatic incurs a *latae sententiae* excommunication, without prejudice to the provision of Canon 194, Par. 1, No. 2; a cleric, moreover, may be punished with the penalties mentioned in Canon 1336 , Par. 1, Nos. 1, 2, and 3." As far as the penalties outlined in Canon 1336, these are additional expiatory penalties that may be imposed, and thus are not directly applicable to the present controversy as neither Lefebvre nor the bishops illicitly consecrated have seriously attempted to reconcile their schism. Therefore, we can ignore Canon 1336 since it does not apply within this context.

On the other hand, the first paragraph of Canon 194 provides that "one who has publicly defected from the catholic faith or from communion with the Church" is "removed from ecclesiastical office by virtue of the law itself." However, the second paragraph of Canon 194 legislates that the "removal mentioned in [Canon 194, Par. 1] Nos. 2 and 3 can be insisted upon only if it is established by declaration of the competent authority."

As the penalties mentioned in the first paragraph of Canon 1364 apply to Lefebvre, he incurred an additional *latae sententiae* excommunication for the offense of schism. Canon 751 defines schism as "the withdrawal of submission to the Supreme Pontiff or from communion with the members of the Church subject to him." Lefebvre's act of consecrating bishops without papal mandate was a refusal of submission to the express will of the Supreme Pontiff. As the penalty for schism was declared by the competent authority in the form of the Holy See, Lefebvre was automatically removed from all ecclesiastical office by virtue of the law itself. Although given the archbishop's previous suspension from priestly faculties, it is debatable whether he in fact held an ecclesiastical office at the time of his excommunication.

Against the declaration of schism, however, Lefebvre's followers have argued that his consecration of bishops without papal mandate was not an act of withdrawal of submission to the Roman Pontiff or from the communion with the Church, but merely an act of disobedience. In citing one canonical study, Lefebvre's followers maintain that "schism, defined in Canon 751, means refusal of subjection to the Supreme Pontiff or refusal of communion with other members of the Church. A mere act of disobedience to a superior does not imply denial that the superior holds office or has authority."

The above argument fails to take into account four variables relevant to Lefebvre's consecration of bishops against the express will of the Supreme Pontiff. First, Canon 751 does not specify that one must deny the superior's possession of authority to incur schism, but rather that one must refuse to submit to this authority. Secondly, the superior to whom Lefebvre refused submission was the Supreme Pontiff, who possesses full ordinary power and universal jurisdiction. Thirdly, the consecration of bishops against the express will of the Supreme Pontiff is no mere act of disobedience, but an act which carries by virtue of the law the penalty of *latae sententiae* excommunication — penalties which, when Lefebvre made public his intention to consecrate bishops without papal mandate, were reiterated to him personally by no less than the Supreme Pontiff and two cardinal prefects of curial congregations.

Finally, in light of Lefebvre's express intention in consecrating bishops without papal mandate, that of providing for the continuation of the SSPX until Rome adopts his position, Lefebvre was not carrying out an isolated act of disobedience, but rather he intended to perpetuate a situation of disobedience for a prolonged period of time. Hence, in light of the above variables, Lefebvre's act of consecrating bishops without papal mandate cannot reasonably be dismissed as a simple, isolated act of disobedience to a superior.

Therefore, an objective canonical analysis of Lefebvre's situation illustrates that he incurred a *latae sententiae* excommunication by virtue of the law both for the act of consecrating bishops without papal mandate, and for carrying out this act against the express will of the Supreme Pontiff as an act of schism. Thus, the canonical arguments proposed by the Lefebvrite movement against the validity of the excommunications cannot be sustained in light of the Church's canonical jurisprudence.

CHAPTER FIVE
After the Excommunication

∽

THE OUTCOME OF THE MOVEMENT promoted by Msgr. Lefebvre can and must be, for all the Catholic faithful, a motive for sincere reflection concerning their own fidelity to the Church's Tradition, authentically interpreted by the ecclesiastical magisterium, ordinary and extraordinary, especially in the Ecumenical Councils from Nicaea to Vatican II. From this reflection, all should draw a renewed and efficacious conviction of the necessity of strengthening still more their fidelity by rejecting erroneous interpretations and arbitrary and unauthorized application of doctrine, liturgy, and discipline.

— POPE JOHN PAUL II (ECCLESIA DEI, 5A)

"With Great Affliction the Church ..."

On July 2, 1988, two days after Lefebvre's episcopal consecrations without papal mandate, Pope John Paul II promulgated an apostolic letter *motu proprio* (on his own personal initiative), entitled *Ecclesia Dei* (See Appendix I). The Holy Father sought to facilitate the reconciliation to the Church of Archbishop Lefebvre's former followers. In addressing Lefebvre's illicit episcopal consecrations, the Holy Father solemnly confirmed both the excommunication of Lefebvre and the existence of his schism as follows:

> In itself, this act was one of disobedience to the Roman Pontiff in a grave matter and of supreme importance for the unity of the Church, such as is the ordination of bishops whereby the apostolic succession is sacramentally perpetuated. Hence, such disobedience — which implies in practice the rejection of the Roman primacy — constitutes a schismatic act. In performing such an act, notwithstanding the formal canonical warning sent to them by the cardinal prefect of the Congregation for Bishops on 17 June last, Msgr. Lefebvre and the priests Bernard Fellay, Bernard Tissier de Mallerais, Richard Williamson, and Alphonso de Galarreta, have incurred the grave penalty of excommunication envisaged by ecclesiastical law.[59]

In light of the Holy Father's confirmation of Lefebvre's schismatic status, many traditionalists responded positively to the Holy Father's invitation to reconcile their situation. In North America, the process of reconciliation had been facilitated even before the schism ensued, when, on the tenth anniversary of Fr. Leonard Feeney's death, one of the more sizable communities he had founded formally regularized their canonical situation with the Church.[60] Unlike Father Feeney, who was reconciled with the Church under the pontificate of Paul VI in 1972,[61] and who remains a popular folk hero among many traditionalists today, Lefebvre died under the censure of excommunication without having reconciled with the Church.

Yet in the period after Lefebvre's excommunication, many of his followers still dispute, both in print and in public debate, the validity of his excommunication because they claim that in consecrating bishops without papal mandate, he was acting under the compulsion of grave fear in a state of emergency,[62] as provided for in Canon 1323, No. 4; and Canon 1324, Par. 1, Nos. 5 and 8.[63] The first canon cited by Lefebvre's apologists, Canon 1323, No. 4, states: "No one is liable to a penalty who, when violating a law or precept acted under the compulsion of grave fear, even if only relative, or by reason of necessity or grave inconvenience, unless, however, the act is intrinsically evil or tends to be harmful to souls."

Similarly, the first paragraph of Canon 1324, Nos. 5 and 8, which is also cited by Lefebvre's apologists state: "The perpetrator of a violation is not exempted from penalty, but the penalty prescribed in the law or precept must be diminished, or a penance substituted in its place, if the offense was committed by one who was compelled by grave fear, even if only relative, or by reason of necessity or grave inconvenience, if the act is intrinsically evil or tends to be harmful to souls; one who erroneously, but culpably, thought that one of the circumstances existed which are mentioned in Canon 1323, Nos. 4 or 5."

There are two subtle differences between these two canons, the first being that in Canon 1323 the penalty is completely excused, whereas in Canon 1324 the penalty is merely diminished. The second difference is that Canon 1323 does not apply if the violation which incurred the penalty is intrinsically evil or harmful to souls, whereas Canon 1324 still applies in such instances. In light of these two canons, Lefebvre's apologists claim that because Lefebvre believed a state of necessity existed in the Church, regardless of whether such a state was justified or not, he acted under grave fear in illicitly consecrating bishops without papal mandate. Therefore, they maintain that regardless of the Holy See's formal declaration to the contrary, Lefebvre did not incur the *latae sententiae* excommunications imposed by Canons 1364 and 1382.

The Lefebvrite argument that Lefebvre acted under grave fear in order to resolve a state of necessity is problematic for many reasons. First of all, to reiterate the principle of the first paragraph of Canon 16, laws are authentically interpreted by the legislator. In the case of Lefebvre, to sustain an argument based upon Canons 1323 and 1324, his followers must maintain that the supreme legislator, which is the Holy Father, has inauthentically interpreted his own law, while Lefebvre somehow came across the authentic interpretation of what the Supreme Pontiff legislated. The contradictory nature of such a position has been noted by the Pontifical Commission for the Interpretation of Legislative Texts in the following statement:

> However, doubt cannot reasonably be cast upon the validity of the excommunication of the bishops declared in the *motu proprio* [*Ecclesia Dei*] and the decree [of excommunication against Lefebvre]. In particular, it does not seem that one may be able to find, as far as the imputability of the penalty is concerned, any exempting or lessening circumstances (Cf. CIC, Canon 1323-1324). As far as the state of necessity in which Msgr. Lefebvre thought to find himself, one must keep before one that such a state must be verified objectively, and there is never a necessity to ordain bishops contrary to the will of the Roman Pontiff, head of the college of bishops. This would, in fact, imply the possibility of "serving" the Church by means of an attempt against its unity in an area connected with the very foundations of this unity.[64]

Therefore, one sees that a state of emergency cannot be invoked against the expressed judgment of the Holy Father, especially on such an important issue as the consecration of bishops. One also sees that the mind of the legislator does not favor the Lefebvrite argument. Therefore, on the basis of the first paragraph of Canon 16, Lefebvre's followers cannot sustain an argument in favor of the illicit consecration of bishops based upon Canons 1323 and 1324. For such an argument ignores the authentic interpretation of the supreme legislator regarding the content of his legislation.

Yet, as most of Lefebvre's followers reject the interpretation of the Supreme Pontiff with regard to the *latae sententiae* excommunication of Lefebvre, the situation must be examined in light of canonical tradition. The second paragraph of Canon 6 dictates, "to the extent that the canons of this [1983] code reproduce the former law, they are to be assessed in the light also of canonical tradition." Under the pontificate of Pius XII, the Sacred Congregation of the Holy Office stated that the former law decrees that grave fear does not mitigate from the penalty of excommunication when one consecrates bishops without papal mandate.[65] This fact refutes the Lefebvrite argument that the "1917 [*Code of*] *Canon Law* inflicted only a suspension" for the act of consecrating bishops without papal mandate.[66] Therefore, under pre-conciliar legislation, the consecration of bishops without papal mandate, even when coerced by grave fear, does not mitigate one from incuring a *latae sententiae* excommunication.

When confronted with this decree from the Holy Office, however, Lefebvre's apologists will argue that it was introduced within the context of the Chinese Patriotic Catholic Church.[67] Yet while the situation in China may have been the catalyst for this decree, there is nothing within it to suggest that it merely binds the particular Church within China. Rather, having received universal promulgation, the text of the decree clearly applies to bishops universally.

Next, some of Lefebvre's followers have argued against the decree from the Holy Office using Canon 6, Par. 1, No. 3, which states: "When this code comes into force, the following are abrogated: all penal laws enacted by the Apostolic See, whether universal or particular, unless they are resumed in this code itself." For whereas the decree from the Holy Office specifically denies coercion from grave fear as a mitigating circumstance in the *latae sententiae* excommunication of those who consecrate bishops without papal mandate, Canon 1382 is silent about coercion due to grave fear. Therefore, some of Lefebvre's apologists have argued a doubt of law vis-à-vis the applicability of the decree from the Holy Office, noting Canon 14 which legislates that "laws, even invalidating and incapacitating ones, do not oblige when there is a doubt of law."

Nevertheless, such an argument is also unsustainable. This is especially the case when we take into account Canon 21, which states that "in doubt, the revocation of a previous law is not presumed; rather, later laws are to be related to earlier ones and, as far as possible, harmonized with them." Hence, Lefebvre's apologists cannot reasonably presume that the previous legislation has been suppressed by the first paragraph of Canon 6 with regard to the mitigating circumstances of those who consecrate bishops without papal mandate under the coercion of grave fear.

In light of the above, Lefebvre's arguments in favor of the mitigation of his *latae sententiae* excommunication based upon Canons 1323 and 1324 stands refuted within the broader context of canonical jurisprudence, and thus cannot reasonably be sustained in light of objective analysis of his situation after the episcopal consecrations without papal mandate.

In concluding this brief history of the schism and excommunication of Archbishop Lefebvre, one sees a schism which took place in various stages. With each passing stage, Lefebvre's followers have presented canonical arguments against the validity of censures incurred by Archbishop Lefebvre and the movement he founded. More often than not, these arguments have sought to isolate particular canons from the wider context of ecclesiastical law as a whole. However, when the canons cited by Lefebvre's apologists are interpreted according to the will of the legislator as well as the wider context of canonical jurisprudence, such arguments as proposed by the Lefebvrite movement are not sustainable. Therefore, one cannot but conclude that Lefebvre's act of consecrating bishops against the express will of the Supreme Pontiff was a schismatic act incurring the *latae sententiae* penalty of excommunication by virtue of the law itself.

In closing, as the Bishop of Rome is the one to whom the Lefebvrite movement refuses submission, the authors would like to remind those who adhere to Lefebvre's schism of the following teaching imparted by St. Paul in his Epistle to the Romans:

> Let every person be subject to the governing authorities. For there is no authority except from God, and those that exist have been instituted by God. Therefore he who resists the authorities resists what God has appointed, and those who resist will incur judgment.[68]

PART TWO

Traditionalists' Claims Against the Second Vatican Council

CHAPTER SIX

Was Vatican II "Merely a Pastoral Council"?

AND JESUS CAME AND SAID to them, "All authority in heaven and on earth has been given to me. Go therefore and make disciples of all nations, baptizing them in the name of the Father and of the Son and of the Holy Spirit, teaching them to observe all that I have commanded you; and lo, I am with you always, to the close of the age."

— MATTHEW 28:18-20

Proponents of extreme Traditionalism will often take refuge behind the claim that Vatican II was "merely a pastoral council," therefore it cannot be recognized as an infallible council. "Didn't the Second Vatican Council, as a merely pastoral council," they demand, "break with Tradition? Furthermore, what infallible statement did Vatican II promulgate?" These are good questions that deserve good answers. The pastoral nature of the Second Vatican Council is the source of much controversy among many traditionalists. In fact, many traditional Catholics who reconcile with the Church continue to wrestle with this question long after their return to the Church.

Fortunately, Fr. Gérald de Servigny answers many of these questions in his book *La Théologie de L'Euchariste dans le Concile Vatican II*, which is currently being translated by one of the authors into the English language. Father de Servigny is a licensed theologian who brings both keen pastoral insight and theological reflection to the question, and this chapter could not have been written without his help. We are grateful to both him and his publisher Pierre Téqui Éditeur for granting us permission to translate and quote freely from his book in this chapter.[69]

Many traditionalists argue that the Second Vatican Council was the first general council of the Church to be uniquely convened as a "pastoral" council. Yet the word "pastoral" can be understood (and misunderstood) in different ways. When applied to the Second Vatican Council, as Father de Servigny points out, the word pastoral must be understood in the context of what Pope John XXIII intended when he convened the Council. This is a fairly common principle when it comes to the interpretation of the sacred sciences. In fact, one can draw a parallel between Father de Servigny's approach and Canon 17 of the 1983 *Code of Canon Law* (or, since the 1983 *Code of Canon Law* was not yet in effect when Pope John XXIII convened the Second Vatican Council, Canon 18 from the 1917 *Code of Canon Law*).

Father de Servigny cites the following paragraph from Pope John XXIII's opening discourse at the Second Vatican Council: "It must come to pass that this certain and immutable doctrine, which must be faithfully respected, is deepened and presented in a way that replies to the demands of our time … We must attach much importance to this way and work patiently, if need be, towards its elaboration, and we must hasten to a way of presenting it that better corresponds to a teaching whose character is pastoral above all else."[70]

This is a fairly good summary of how Pope John XXIII understood the word *pastoral* when he convened the Second Vatican Council as a pastoral council. Pastoral does *not* mean that the Second Vatican Council merely focused upon the Church's pastoral discipline — those laws and practices subject to change over time. Nor does pastoral mean the Second Vatican Council ignored the Church's teaching, since its pronouncements had to be based upon some previous Catholic teaching in order to qualify as one of the Church's general councils. Rather, pastoral in this context means taking the Church's existing, immutable teaching — those matters of faith and morals that we derive from Holy Scripture and Sacred Tradition — and putting them into practice in a manner that challenges today's society and culture in terms it can comprehend.

"While the temptation exists to oppose the Second Vatican Council's pastoral nature with the dogmatic nature of previous ecumenical councils," Father de Servigny warns, "pastoral and dogmatic do not automatically exclude one another. For a pastoral teaching is a theological teaching, albeit not purely intellectual and reserved to theologians. Rather, it is transmitted to the everyday world in order to spiritually feed Christians and enlighten them about the mystery of God. It is this teaching that enlightens the faithful, telling us what we must believe and what we must do to grow in our relationship with our Lord Jesus Christ."

In other words, *pastoral* determines where a doctrine stands among the average Catholic in the pew. We don't study God for God's sake, but for our own. We study the mystery of God to better understand Him, to love Him all the more, and to live His truth more fully. For instance, doctrinal theology teaches us about the great mystery of Christ's redemption, whereas pastoral theology teaches us to put this mystery into practice by frequenting the sacrament of confession. Doctrinal theology teaches us about the mystery of transubstantiation during the holy Sacrifice of the Mass, whereas pastoral theology teaches us when we can and cannot partake of this mystery.

Once the reader understands this pastoral orientation of the Second Vatican Council, Father de Servigny introduces the following quotation from Cardinal Yves Congar, O.P. — one of the many theological experts invited to partake in the Council. "What John XXIII designated by pastoral was doctrine," Cardinal Congar writes, "but expressing itself in history, in the time of the actual world ... It is doctrinal, but pastoral doctrine, that is to say doctrine that asks to be applied historically."[71] What Congar means is that, as a pastoral council, the Second Vatican Council sought to apply the Church's teaching within the context of current history — to make the Church's doctrine relevant to today's world. At the incarnation, Christ didn't merely take upon Himself human flesh — He also took upon Himself our customs, mores, culture, and, as far as creation is concerned, time and space. Thus, doctrine applies here and now, across the expanse of human geography, in an age of modern technology and universal communications. Doctrine is not simply restricted to the Hebrew population gathered in the vicinity of Jerusalem during the era of King Herod and Pontius Pilate.

Father de Servigny writes:

> For Congar and for others, pastoral doctrine is an incarnate doctrine, not unlike our Lord who incarnated Himself in the womb of the Blessed Virgin. Its vocabulary also possesses the ability to renew itself. For while the Church's essential teaching can't change according to the time or the culture,

the Church can render this teaching more accessible to the faithful according to time and place, as she discovers better ways of expressing the essential truths of our Faith.

Therefore, we shouldn't mistake pastoral for negligible, secondary, or meaningless, nor should we see it as inferior to the magisterial or to purely doctrinal teaching. Yet this is how certain opposition movements have come to misunderstand the Council, always in order to combat it. To briefly summarize their arguments, they oppose the pastoral character of the Vatican Council because they maintain that as a pastoral council, Vatican II only undertook a disciplinary content. Following up on this faulty premise, they then conclude the Second Vatican Council obviously had nothing to do with the magisterial teaching of the Church.

Father de Servigny then points us to the following insights penned by Pope Paul VI in a letter responding to Archbishop Lefebvre's criticism of certain conciliar texts. "You cannot invoke the distinction between dogmatic and pastoral in order to accept certain texts of the Council and to refute others," the Holy Father explains. "Certainly, all that was said in the Council does not demand an assent of the same nature, only that which is affirmed as an object of faith or truth attached to the faith, by definitive acts, require an assent of faith. But the rest is also a part of the solemn magisterium of the Church to which all faithful must make a confident reception and a sincere application."[72]

Thus, even the purely pastoral teaching of the Second Vatican Council belongs to the Church's magisterium. After all, the three functions of the Church are to teach, to govern, and to sanctify. While each of these functions is unique — much as the Father, the Son, and the Holy Ghost exist as unique persons within the Holy Trinity — they are nevertheless inter-related. Similarly, the Church's purely doctrinal teaching is related to how this teaching is implemented. In other words, the Church's governing function can never be totally separated from her teaching function. And thus the Second Vatican Council's pronouncements are at the same time both doctrinal and pastoral.

Father de Servigny speaks of the consequences this implies:

> The Supreme Pontiff and the bishops gathered into a council, and subsequently the Holy Spirit assists the college of bishops, as successors of the Holy Apostles, in proposing doctrine to the universal Church. Of notable interest is the formula employed by the Holy Father and the bishops in signing and promulgating the text, namely: "by virtue of the apostolic power that we hold from Christ in union with the venerable fathers, we approve, decree, and establish in the Holy Spirit …"

While the weight of each particular text arising from the Second Vatican Council may vary, the documents are nevertheless to be received and understood as authoritative Church teaching. The pastoral texts of the Second Vatican Council carry behind them the weight of college of bishops teaching in communion with the Roman Pontiff. As we read in *Pastor Aeternus*, the First Vatican Council's Dogmatic Constitution on the Church,

> To him, in blessed Peter, full power has been given by our Lord Jesus Christ to tend, rule, and govern the universal Church. All this is to be found in the acts of the ecumenical councils and the sacred canons … Both clergy and faith-

ful, of whatever rite and dignity ... are bound to submit to this power by the duty of hierarchical subordination and true obedience, and this not only in matters concerning faith and morals, but also in those which regard the discipline and government of the Church throughout the world.

In short, Catholic Tradition maintains we must submit to the Roman Pontiff in matters of discipline and governance, which encompass the pastoral application of doctrine, and not merely in faith and morals. As Catholics, we cannot become like Martin Luther, who at the Diet of Worms, allegedly stated, "I do not accept the authority of popes and councils for they have contradicted each other."

At this point, it is helpful to look at the doctrine the Second Vatican Council attempted to put into pastoral practice. "From the very first lines of *Lumen Gentium*, Vatican II's Dogmatic Constitution on the Church," Father de Servigny writes, "the Council places itself in continuity with previous ecumenical councils. Witness the following statement within the opening paragraph of *Lumen Gentium*: '[The Church] here proposes, for the benefit of the faithful and of the whole world, to set forth, as clearly as possible, and in the Tradition laid down by earlier Councils, her own nature and universal mission.'"

This claim may seem incredible to some of his fellow traditionalists, but Father de Servigny backs it up with hard information. In terms of quantity, the Second Vatican Council abundantly cites its two immediate predecessors — namely, the Council of Trent and the First Vatican Council. In fact, each of these councils is substantially cited twenty times in the Second Vatican Council.[73] "The first reference to the Council of Trent appears in the fifty-fifth paragraph of *Sacrosanctum Concilium* (Vatican II's Constitution on the Sacred Liturgy)," Father de Servigny shares, "with regard to communion under both species: 'The dogmatic principles which were laid down by the Council of Trent remaining intact …'" This is a most important reference to a prior council since it establishes a concrete area where the Second Vatican Council is to be interpreted in light of the Council of Trent. In short, the doctrinal principles underlying the pastoral focus of the Second Vatican Council are those of the Council of Trent.

CHAPTER SEVEN

Vatican II and the Holy Eucharist

AFTER THIS MANY OF HIS DISCIPLES drew back and no longer went about with him. Jesus said to the twelve, "Will you also go away?" Simon Peter answered him, "Lord, to whom shall we go? You have the words of eternal life."

— JOHN 6:66–67

A Weakened Sense of Our Lord's Presence?

A common charge perpetuated by many extreme traditionalists is that the Second Vatican Council and the Church's subsequent liturgical reform weakened the faith of Catholics in the Holy Eucharist and the Real Presence. Some state that this was intentional, alleging various outside conspiracies by the Church's enemies, while others feel that this is a byproduct of the Church's attempt to reach out to Protestants and other non-Catholics. As the arguments and their underlying reasons are legion, it would be impossible in a small work such as this to address and refute each and every objection raised by the schismatic or suspicious traditionalist. Rather, it is much easier to simply present a brief overview of what the Second

Vatican Council, and subsequently Pope Paul VI, taught concerning the Holy Eucharist.

Responding to modernist abuses that arose after the Second Vatican Council, a wise Benedictine theologian once said to one of the authors: "Those who quote the spirit of Vatican II have seldom read the documents." These words apply equally to those traditionalists who feel that the Second Vatican Council undermined the Church's traditional Eucharistic theology. For from the opening paragraphs of the Second Vatican Council, one discovers a renewed emphasis on the Holy Eucharist as the central focus in the Church's prayer life. In fact this Eucharistic foundation first comes to light in the following excerpt from the tenth paragraph of *Sacrosanctum Concilium*, the Council's Constitution on the Sacred Liturgy:

> From the Liturgy, therefore, and especially from the Eucharist, as from a fountain, grace is channeled into us; and the sanctification of men in Christ and the glorification of God, to which all other activities of the Church are directed as toward their goal, are most powerfully achieved.

Within this statement, one clearly sees the intention of the conciliar fathers to recognize the Eucharist as the center of the Church's devotional life. Within the Liturgy, the Eucharist is encouraged among the faithful as the fountain from which grace is drawn, and the end towards which all other acts of Catholic devotion are directed.

An image we can use to explain the Second Vatican Council's theology of the Eucharist is that of a fountain on a mountain. The fountain, of course, is our Lord Jesus Christ who is the source of all life. Our life is a spiritual pilgrimage in which we climb the mountain, seeking to come closer to this fountain which lay on the summit. Yet mountain climbing is strenuous exercise; we no doubt will become thirsty along the way. We need not fear such thirst, however, since the fountain is also the source of refreshing streams of pure water that will satiate our thirst along the way.

In short, Vatican II teaches us that as Catholics we derive our spiritual strength principally from the Eucharist. Additionally, our purpose in fulfilling all other devotions within the Church's spiritual treasury is to draw closer to Christ's Real Presence in the Most Holy Sacrament of the Eucharist. Thus, despite the claims to the contrary raised by many extreme traditionalists, the Holy Eucharist is a theme that consistently surfaces throughout each of the Second Vatican Council's documents.

Witness the following passage from the Council's Dogmatic Constitution on the Church, *Lumen Gentium*:

> Each must share frequently in the sacraments, the Eucharist especially, and in liturgical rites. Each must apply himself constantly to prayer, self-denial, active brotherly service, and the exercise of all virtues. For charity, as the bond of perfection and the fulfillment of the law (Cf. Col. 3:14; Rom. 13:10), rules over all the means of attaining holiness, gives life to them, and makes them work. [Par. 42]

As one reads in this passage, the Second Vatican Council exhorts all Catholics to partake of the sacraments frequently, particularly the Eucharist, which the Council has already taught us is the source and the summit of the spiritual life. Thus the Second Vatican Council calls us to perfect the virtue of charity through frequent reception of the sacraments, particularly the Holy Eucharist. From the teaching of St. Paul in the New Testament, we know charity to be the most important virtue, the virtue without which all our other acts of piety are meaningless. Charity is perfected through the reception of the Eucharist and the other sacraments in a worthy manner, and through this same action we grow in holiness.

This is an important passage to keep in mind. It demonstrates the emphasis placed by the fathers of the Second Vatican Council on frequent reception of the sacraments, especially Holy Communion and confession, when it comes to living a life of holiness. Clearly, the Church at Vatican II never intended, as some traditionalists claim, to do away with the sacraments as well as the Church's rich treasury of sacramentals. Rather, exactly the opposite is true. While Vatican II encouraged Catholics to engage the world, it did so in the context of a regular life of prayer, self-sacrifice, and frequent reception of the sacraments.

Yet the Council goes much further than these basic prescriptions in its document *Unitatis Redintegratio*, its Decree on Ecumenism. Charity unites men with God, as well as Christians with one another. As the sacrament of Communion, the Holy Eucharist is by that very fact the sacrament of unity. One would expect this to be expressed within the Second Vatican Council's Eucharistic teaching, and the Council does so within the context of ecumenism as follows:

> Before offering Himself up as a spotless victim upon the altar of the cross, He prayed to His Father for those who believe: "That they may all be one; even as thou, Father, art in me, and I in thee, that they also may be one in us, so that the world may believe that thou hast sent me" (John 17:21). In His Church He instituted the wonderful sacrament of the

Eucharist by which the unity of the Church is both signified and brought about. [Par. 2]

Far from selling out the Church's traditional theology for the sake of ecumenism and better relations with non-Catholic Christians, the Second Vatican Council clearly teaches that the Holy Eucharist is the sacrament through which the unity of the Church is both signified and brought about. By "both signified and brought about," the Church is emphasizing that the Eucharist is the sign of unity within the Church, meaning that the Eucharist signifies the unity of Catholic believers both with God and with each other. However, the Eucharist also brings about this unity which is signified, gathering the faithful into one body, the Church, and uniting us with God the Father through the reception of Christ's Body and Blood. As such, the Eucharist is a foretaste of what awaits the believer in heaven, when united with other believers he will behold in all His glory.[74]

The message of the Second Vatican Council is clear: Without the Holy Eucharist, there can be no unity among Christians. This deep Eucharistic theme permeates the various texts of the Second Vatican Council. Nowhere is this more noticeable than in *Presbyterorum Ordinis*, the Second Vatican Council's Decree on the Ministry and Life of Priests. This is important to keep in mind since many traditionalists also argue that the Second Vatican Council weakened the relationship between the sacramental priesthood and the Holy Eucharist, as well as the connection between the local church community and the Holy Eucharist. Yet as the following excerpt from *Presbyterorum Ordinis* shows, this was not the intention of the Second Vatican Council:

No Christian community, however, can be built up unless it has its basis and center in the celebration of the most Holy Eucharist. Here, therefore, all education in the spirit of community must originate. If this celebration is to be sincere and thorough, it must lead to various works of charity and mutual help, as well as to missionary activity and to different forms of Christian witness. [Par. 6]

To reiterate a theme which has become consistent throughout the teachings of the Second Vatican Council, the Eucharist is the center of the Church. The Eucharist and the Mass are also the center of the local parish community — not only in devotional matters, but in catechetical and educational matters as well. The various other actions of the Church, including corporal works of mercy and missionary apostolate, derive their spiritual foundation from the Holy Eucharist. These latter works, the Council assures us, are the fruits of a sincere Eucharistic faith.

Admittedly, the Church witnessed many abuses in this area after the Second Vatican Council. Many local parishes did away with Eucharistic devotions and de-emphasized the centrality of the Holy Eucharist while placing an undue amount of emphasis upon social justice and the corporal works of mercy. This was often done in the spirit of exaggerated inclusivity, in the name of ecumenism toward our separated Protestant brethren, and in an effort to become more engaging toward an unbelieving world. The catchwords from this era are as legion as the abuses they wrought, and traditionalists — whether in communion with Rome or of the schismatic variety — rightly complain about them. Most were simply confused, their concerns often not taken seriously at the time by the Church's hierarchy.

Nevertheless, one must separate these abuses from the authentic intention of the Council. The intention of the conciliar fathers is clear: Within the local Church community, Catholic action, and in fact all of the Church's ministry and apostolate, flows from a deep Eucharistic faith. Nowhere is this insight more clearly stated than in the following paragraph of *Presbyterorum Ordinis*:

> The other sacraments, as well as every ministry of the Church and every work of the apostolate, are linked with the Holy Eucharist and are directed toward it. For the most blessed Eucharist contains the Church's entire spiritual wealth, that is, Christ Himself, our Passover and living bread. Through His very flesh, made vital and vitalizing by the Holy Spirit, He offers life to men. They are thereby invited and led to offer themselves, their labors, and all created things together with him. [Par. 5]

Basically, this paragraph nicely summarizes the Church's universal call to holiness at the Second Vatican Council, through which we receive as faithful Catholics a radical invitation to make the Eucharist the source and the summit of our spiritual lives as Catholics. Every work of the apostolate, as well as all other sacraments, are intrinsically linked to the Holy Eucharist, the spiritual end towards which they are directed. All of Catholic action recommended to us from Holy Scripture and Tradition is contained in the Holy Eucharist, which is the very Body and Blood of our Lord present within our midst today, and without which there can be no life in the spiritual sense. Far from denying the Church's traditional Eucharistic theology, the Second Vatican Council seeks to put it into pastoral practice.

This includes the sacrificial aspect of the Church's traditional Eucharistic theology. Despite what some traditionalists claim, at the Second Vatican Council the Church did not shy away from — let alone suppress — the central focus of the Eucharist within our Church. Jesus Christ, as the Church has always maintained, is truly present in the most Holy Eucharist. Through the Mass, He offers Himself up to God the Father as an unbloody sacrifice. *Presbyterorum Ordinis* reaffirms these traditional teachings as follows:

> Thus the Eucharistic action is the very heartbeat of the congregation of the faithful over which the priest presides. So priests must instruct them to offer to God the Father the divine victim in the Sacrifice of the Mass, and to join to it the offering of their own lives. [Par. 5]

Because the Mass is the heartbeat of the local Church community, it follows that our churches, as houses of prayer, must center around the Eucharist. *Presbyterorum Ordinis* reiterates this point in the following manner:

> In the house of prayer, the most Holy Eucharist is celebrated and preserved. There the faithful gather, and find help and comfort through venerating the presence of the Son of God our Savior, offered us on the sacrificial altar. This house must be well-kept and suitable for prayer and sacred action. There, priests and the faithful are called to respond with grateful hearts to the gift of Him who through His humanity constantly pours divine life into the members of His body. [Par. 5]

In light of all these citations from the Second Vatican Council, we see that the Council intended to center the Church around the Eucharist. And nowhere is this more clear than in the following invitation of *Ad Gentes*, the Second Vatican Council's Decree on the Missionary Activity of the Church. Priests are to consecrate themselves to the service of the Holy Eucharist. For through the Eucharist all priests lead the faithful in joining themselves with the Church's missionary zeal:

> Priests represent Christ, and are collaborators with the order of bishops in that threefold sacred task which by its very nature bears on the mission of the Church. Therefore, they should fully understand that their life has also been consecrated to the service of the missions. By means of their own ministry, which deals principally with the Eucharist as the source of perfecting the Church, they are in communion with Christ the head and are leading others to this communion. Hence, they cannot help realizing how much is yet wanting to the fullness of that body, and how much therefore must be done if it is to grow from day to day. [Par. 39]

This paragraph beautifully summarizes the Eucharistic foundation of the Second Vatican Council, relating this most holy sacrament to the Church's three-fold mission of proclaiming the Gospel, sanctifying the faithful, and governing the order and the discipline of the Church. For through the Eucharist, the ministry of the priesthood through which we are sanctified, the hierarchy of the Church through which we are governed, and the missionary action of the Church through which the Gospel is preached, are brought together in order to perfect the Church. In short, the Second Vatican Council summarizes the effects of the Holy Eucharist as the source and summit of the Catholic spiritual life. In such a light, the Church's missionary zeal is nothing more than an attempt to bring the non-Catholic into the Catholic Church, so that they may share in this Eucharistic faith and draw strength from our Lord's Real Presence.

Did Pope Paul VI Compromise or "Water Down" Catholic Teaching on the Real Presence?

Despite the strong reaffirmation of the Church's traditional Eucharistic doctrine at the Second Vatican Council, certain Eucharistic heresies nevertheless emerged around the time of the Council. Certain radical traditionalists are tempted to blame this resurgence on Pope Paul VI who presided over most of the Council. Of course, Pope Paul VI broke with many customs during his pontificate. One incident in particular that comes to mind is the promulgation of a papal encyclical during the time of the Second Vatican Council. The Roman Pontiff may exercise his power collegially, as he does during an ecumenical council, or he may exercise his power personally, such as when he promulgates a papal encyclical. Prior to the Second Vatican Council, it was inconceivable that a Roman Pontiff would interrupt the collegial exercise of his teaching authority to promulgate Church teaching through the personal exercise of his teaching authority.

But on the Feast of Pope St. Pius X in September of 1965, Pope Paul VI interrupted the Second Vatican Council to promulgate his papal encyclical *Mysterium Fidei*. In so doing he intended to uphold the Church's theological Tradition when it came to the Holy Eucharist as well as condemn any false teaching concerning the Eucharist that had begun to surface. For the Catholic seriously seeking to understand the Second Vatican Council, *Mysterium Fidei* provides the key for unlocking the authentic interpretation of this Council in light of the Church's Sacred Tradition. One readily sees this in *Mysterium Fidei*'s opening paragraph, where Paul VI introduces the Catholic faithful to mind of the conciliar fathers as follows:

> The Catholic Church has always devoutly guarded as a most precious treasure the mystery of faith, that is, the ineffable gift of the Eucharist which she received from Christ her spouse as a pledge of His immense love, and during the Second Vatican Council in a new and solemn demonstration, she professed her faith and veneration for this mystery. When dealing with the restoration of the sacred Liturgy, the fathers of the Council, by reason of their pastoral concern for the whole Church, considered it of the highest importance to exhort the faithful to participate actively with sound faith and with the utmost devotion in the celebration of this most holy mystery, to offer it with the priest to God as a sacrifice for their own salvation and for that of the whole world, and to find in it spiritual nourishment.

In essence, at the Second Vatican Council the Church sought not to deny the holy mystery of the Mass, but to safeguard its central role in the sanctification of Christ's faithful. Along with the other fathers of the Second Vatican Council, Paul VI considers active lay participation in the Holy Eucharist of the utmost importance. Furthermore, he reaffirms the sacrificial aspect the Mass in which our Lord's Real Presence is offered up to God the Father for the salvation of the individual and of the whole world. In fact, he goes on to state:

> For if the sacred Liturgy holds the first place in the life of the Church, the Eucharistic mystery stands at the heart and

center of the Liturgy, since it is the font of life by which we are cleansed and strengthened to live not for ourselves but for God, and to be united in love among ourselves.

In short, the Liturgy holds first place in the Church, for the Liturgy is the Church's public prayer whereby the faithful, as Christ's mystical body, unite with Christ their head in order to offer worship to God the Father. As Christ's Body, Blood, Soul, and Divinity is substantially present under the accidents of bread and wine, the Eucharist stands at the heart of the Liturgy. What distinguishes the Eucharist from the other sacraments is that Christ is truly present in being and not merely in action. As Christ's Real Presence, Paul VI places the Eucharist (and rightly so!) at the center of our spiritual lives as Catholics, through which God the Son is offered to God the Father in atonement for our human sins. Thus in conformity with both Holy Scripture and Tradition, Paul VI feels inspired to state:

> In these words are highlighted both the sacrifice, which pertains to the essence of the Mass which is celebrated daily, and the sacrament in which the faithful participate in Holy Communion by eating the Flesh of Christ and drinking His Blood, receiving both grace, the beginning of eternal life, and the medicine of immortality. According to the words of our Lord: "The man who eats my flesh and drinks my blood enjoys eternal life, and I will raise him up at the last day."

What one notices here is that Pope Paul VI pays particular attention to Christ's Real Presence in the most holy sacrament of the Eucharist, a teaching of the Church to which he goes through great pain to substantiate from the Church's theological Tradition. This is consistent throughout the work. For example, in the following passage Paul VI upholds the Real Presence by referring to the teachings of a long chain of Tradition. Pope Paul VI cites St. Thomas Aquinas' use of a quotation taken from the Patristic Father St. Cyril commenting upon a passage of St. Luke's Gospel account of Jesus Christ at the Last Supper:

> The scholastic doctors often made similar affirmations: That in this sacrament are the true Body of Christ and His true Blood is something that "cannot be apprehended by the senses," says St. Thomas, "but only by faith which relies on divine authority. This is why, in a comment on Luke 22:19 ('This is my body which is given for you'), St. Cyril says: 'Do not doubt whether this is true, but rather receive the words of the Savior in faith, for since He is the truth, He cannot lie.'"

As one can see from this quotation, not only has Paul VI staunchly upheld the Traditional Catholic doctrines of transubstantiation and the Real Presence, but he has carefully shown all the golden links in the chain of Tradition which continue throughout the Second Vatican Council. In short, the teachings passed down from Christ to His apostles through the Patristic Fathers and the scholastic doctors find voice in the teachings of Pope Paul VI and the Second Vatican Council.

In fact Christ's Real Presence in the Holy Eucharist, which we are called to consume, cannot but be the teaching of the Catholic Church. For to whom can Paul VI turn as the visible head of Christ's mystical body if not the invisible head who is Jesus Christ? The teaching of Tradition passed down by Christ to His apostles, as Paul VI explains in the following passage, is the only position the Church may preach vis-à-vis the Eucharist:

> Moreover, the Holy Gospel alludes to this when it tells of the many disciples of Christ who, after listening to the sermon about eating His Flesh and drinking His Blood, turned away and left our Lord, saying, "This is a hard saying, who can listen to it?" (John 6:60). Peter, on the other hand, in reply to Jesus' question whether also the twelve wished to leave, expressed his faith and that of the others promptly and resolutely with the marvelous answer: "Lord, to whom shall we go? You have the words of eternal life" (John 6:68).

As an aside, what is of interest to note in the above citation taken from holy Scripture is that when all others have abandoned the Savior because of the difficulty of his teaching, St. Peter is the one who turns to our Lord, and on behalf of the apostles answers those who find our Lord's teachings too difficult, asking rhetorically "To whom shall we go?" In the face of apostasy, St. Peter is the one who upholds the words of our Lord as "the words of eternal life." In short, against the unbelief of the world, St. Peter upholds Christ's teaching concerning the Real Presence. Could any less have been expected of St. Peter's successor Paul VI when the same Eucharistic doubts arose around the period of the Second Vatican Council? Obviously the answer is no, which is why Pope Paul VI through *Mysterium Fidei* diligently defended our Lord's Eucharistic teachings.

Some traditionalists complain that Paul VI's defense of the Church's Eucharistic teachings was unsuccessful because there remains a Eucharistic crisis within the Church — but how successful was St. Peter in bringing back those who abandoned

Christ in the above Gospel account? Like his predecessor St. Peter, in the face of mass apostasy Pope Paul VI could only uphold the teachings of Christ and leave the rest to our Lord's capacity to work His grace in the hardened hearts of men.

Nevertheless, the extreme traditionalist responds: "The Second Vatican Council *changed* the language of the Eucharistic mystery as well as that of the holy Sacrifice of the Mass!" Granted, this is a strange phenomenon taking place within the Church which one cannot ignore, but Pope Paul VI did not ignore it.

In fact, speaking on behalf of the Church in *Mysterium Fidei*, Paul VI addressed this problem directly with the following solemn warning against those who would tamper with the Church's traditional doctrinal formulation concerning the Holy Eucharist:

The Church, therefore, with the long labor of centuries, and, not without the help of the Holy Spirit, has established a rule of language and confirmed it with the authority of the councils. This rule, which has more than once been the watchword and banner of orthodox faith, must be religiously preserved, and let no one presume to change it at his own pleasure or under the pretext of new science. Who would ever tolerate that the dogmatic formulas used by ecumenical councils for the mysteries of the Holy Trinity and the Incarnation be judged as no longer appropriate for men of our times and therefore that others be rashly substituted for them? *In the same way it cannot be tolerated that any individual should on his own authority modify the formulas which were used by the Council of Trent to express belief in the Eucharistic mystery.* For these formulas, like the others which the Church uses to propose the dogmas of faith, express concepts which are not tied to a certain form of human culture, nor to a specific phase of human culture, nor to one or other theological school (emphasis added).

Furthermore, as we see in the following passage, Pope Paul VI has not ignored those who would reduce the Real Presence to a meaningless doctrinal formula or a mere symbol of the reality of Christ's true presence. Rather, he continues to uphold the teaching of the Church concerning this matter, providing a clear link with Tradition through both references to Holy Scripture and the Patristic Fathers:

While the Eucharistic symbolism brings us to an understanding of the effect proper to this Sacrament, which is the unity of the mystical body, it does not indicate or explain what it is that makes this sacrament different from all others. The constant teaching which the Catholic Church passes on to her catechumens, the understanding of the Christian people, the doctrine defined by the Council of Trent, the very words used by Christ when He instituted the most Holy Eucharist, compel us to acknowledge that "the Eucharist is that flesh of Our Savior Jesus Christ who suffered for our sins and whom the Father in His loving-kindness raised again." To these words of St. Ignatius of Antioch, we may add those which Theodore of Mopsueta, a faithful witness to the faith of the Church on this point, addressed to the faithful: "The Lord did not say, 'This is a *symbol* of My body, and this is a *symbol* of My blood,' but, 'This is My body and My blood.' He teaches us not to look to the nature of those things which lie before us and are perceived by the senses, for by the prayer of thanksgiving and the words spoken over them, they have been changed into flesh and blood" (emphasis added).

Lest any doubt remain in the hearts of the faithful as to what belief concerning the Real Presence the fathers of the Second Vatican Council upheld, Paul VI reaffirms the Council of Trent's definition of transubstantiation within the following passage of *Mysterium Fidei*:

> The Council of Trent, basing itself on this faith of the Church, "openly and sincerely professes that within the holy sacrament of the Eucharist, after the consecration of the bread and wine, our Lord Jesus Christ, true God and true man, is really, truly, and substantially contained under those outward appearances."

While such a strong profession of the Church's traditional Eucharistic teaching may be well and good from a theological viewpoint, Paul VI nevertheless feels that pastoral action must be taken as well to counter various Eucharistic heresies that arose around the time of the Second Vatican Council. Therefore, in *Mysterium Fidei* Pope Paul VI renews the following solemn exhortation of his predecessors Pius VI and Pius XII to all priests:

> After the Council of Trent, our predecessor, Pius VI, on the occasion of the errors of the Synod of Pistoia, warned parish priests, when carrying out their office of teaching, not to neglect to speak of transubstantiation, one of the articles of faith. Similarly our predecessor of happy memory, Pius XII, recalled the bounds which those who undertake to discuss the mystery of transubstantiation might not cross. We ourselves also, in fulfillment of our apostolic office, have openly borne solemn witness to the faith of the Church at the National Eucharistic Congress held recently at Pisa.

In short, as part of the Second Vatican Council renewal of the Church he envisioned, Pope Paul VI renewed the obligation on parish priests to present the Church's teaching on transubstantiation when carrying out their priestly ministry among Christ's faithful. In so doing, he cites the Council of Trent as well as his predecessors within the Petrine succession in order to show continuity with the Church's Tradition.

Clearly, Pope Paul VI did not in the slightest abolish or water down the Church's teaching concerning Christ's Real Presence and transubstantiation. Nor did he weaken or downplay the Church's Tradition vis-à-vis the holy Sacrifice of the Mass. Rather, in *Mysterium Fidei* he firmly upheld the Church's various doctrinal formulations on the Eucharist — oftentimes going to great pain to show continuity with divine Tradition — formulations which he held to be the key for interpreting the texts of the Second Vatican Council. In the end, the Church may have entered into a Eucharistic crisis after the Second Vatican Council. But such a crisis cannot be attributed to Pope Paul VI, who did his part to uphold Church Tradition and combat the various Eucharistic heresies that had sprung up.

Therefore, *Mysterium Fidei* is Pope Paul VI's battle cry to all faithful Catholics, calling us to gather around the Real Presence in the most holy Sacrament of the Eucharist. Unfortunately, very few extreme traditionalists, it seems, have actually read this important document.

CHAPTER EIGHT

Vatican II and Ecumenism

∽

I DO NOT PRAY FOR THESE ONLY, but also for those who believe in me through their word, that they may all be one; even as thou, Father, art in me, and I in thee, that they also may be in us, so that the world may believe that thou hast sent me. The glory which thou hast given me I have given to them, that they may be one even as we are one, I in them and thou in me, that they may become perfectly one.

— JOHN 17:20-23

A number of traditionalists assume that the Second Vatican Council contradicted Church Tradition in its teachings on ecumenism. If this assumption is correct, then the Catholic Church has a serious problem: Vatican II could not be legitimate, since a legitimate ecumenical council may develop but may not contradict the earlier dogmatic teaching of the Church. To address the issue, of course, we must look at how the fathers of the Second Vatican Council understood ecumenism. Basically, most the Council's teaching concerning this matter is contained in *Unitatis Redintegratio*, which is the Council's Decree on Ecumenism. This document opens with the following paragraph:

> The restoration of unity among all Christians is one of the principal concerns of the Second Vatican Council. Christ the Lord founded one Church and one Church only. However, many Christian communions present themselves to men as the true inheritors of Jesus Christ; all indeed profess to be followers of the Lord but they differ in mind and go their different ways, as if Christ himself were divided. [Cf. 1 Cor 1:13] Certainly, such division openly contradicts the will of Christ, scandalizes the world, and damages that most holy cause, the preaching of the Gospel to every creature.

Ecumenism concerns the relationship between Christians who fall within different Churches and ecclesiastical communions. Its purpose is to help bring about the restoration of Christian unity, recognizing that Christ only founded one Church. Ecumenism is thus spiritual dialogue and activity in which the Catholic Church engages other Christians. "Other Christians" is traditionally understood to mean validly baptized non-Catholics. This means, for example, that Catholic-Orthodox dialogue or Catholic-Anglican dialogue constitutes ecumenism, because both Anglicans and the Orthodox are validly baptized non-Catholic Christians.

Ecumenism doesn't, however, cover Catholic-Islamic dialogue or Catholic-Hindu dialogue, because Muslims and Hindus, obviously, are not Christian. The Church describes this kind of spiritual activity with non-Christian religions as "interfaith dialogue." The conciliar fathers covered this subject in

Nostra Aetate, which is the Second Vatican Council's Declaration on the Relation of the Church to Non-Christian Religions. This is important to keep in mind, since many traditionalists complain about "ecumenism with Hindus and Buddhists" or some other non-Christian world religion, which is a misunderstanding of the meaning of ecumenism.

This is where another distinction must be drawn in the terms employed by the fathers of the Second Vatican Council. Generally, when the documents speak of "other Churches," they are referring to Eastern non-Catholic Churches that have preserved all seven sacraments, namely, the Eastern Orthodox Churches, the Oriental Orthodox Churches, and the Assyrian Churches of the East. Subsequent ecclesiastical documents have also employed the term "Eastern non-Catholic Churches or their equivalent in law." This broadened definition includes all Eastern non-Catholic Churches as well as such ecclesiastical entities that have preserved the seven sacraments, such as the Polish National Catholic Church, the Chinese Patriotic Catholic Church, and the historical Old Catholic Churches; and, in the future, we will likely see the Society of St. Pius X added to this category.

On the other hand, Protestants and other Christian bodies that have not, in the estimation of the Catholic Church, preserved apostolic succession and consequently the ability to validly administer all seven sacraments, fall into the category of "ecclesial communities." The Catholic Church includes the Anglican Communion, despite their historic protest, in this latter category of "ecclesial community."

Additionally, on the topic of definitions, we should note that the conciliar fathers distinguish between *communicatio in sacris* and *communicatio in spiritualibus* in their teachings. On May 14, 1967, the Secretariat for the Promotion of Unity of

Christians promulgated *Ad Totam Ecclesiam*, in which it defined these two terms as follows: "The term *communicatio in spiritualibus* (sharing of spiritual activity and resources) is used to cover all prayer offered in common, common use of sacred places and objects [e.g. the Bible] ... There is *communicatio in sacris* (sharing of sacraments) when anyone takes part in the liturgical worship or in the sacraments of another church or ecclesial community." In practical terms, *communicatio in sacris* applies to the ecumenical sharing of the sacraments, whereas *communicatio in spiritualibus* applies to the ecumenical sharing of all other spiritual activity.

Generally, the Church encourages *communicatio in spiritualibus* between Catholics and Protestants, but strictly limits *communicatio in sacris* to a handful of sacraments, and even then only between Catholics and members of an Eastern non-Catholic Church. See, for instance, Canon 844 of the current *Code of Canon Law*. Under certain circumstances, Catholics may share in the sacraments of confession, Holy Communion and anointing of the sick with members of Eastern non-Catholic Churches or their equivalent in law. These circumstances, while well-defined, are not overly restrictive. Nevertheless, in keeping with the canon, "the danger of error or indifferentism [must be] avoided ..."

The Spirit of Ecumenical Dialogue

Admittedly, the Church has seen abuses in the name of ecumenism since the closing of the Second Vatican Council. SSPX adherents are familiar with many of these abuses, and they often blame such abuses on the Council itself. They believe ecumenical dialogue waters down the Church's doctrine and must necessarily lead to the heresy of religious indifferentism (the idea that differences in religion are essentially unimportant). A few even argue that ecumenism itself is heresy. They think ecumenism must necessarily entail a watering down of the Catholic Church's traditional teaching that she alone is the Church founded by Christ — that she alone is the Ark of Salvation under the New Covenant.

In making such charges, these individuals fail to take into account the Church's perennial Tradition. *Reconciliatio et Paenitentia*, Pope John Paul II's apostolic exhortation on reconciliation and penance, both addresses and clarifies where the Church stands concerning ecumenical dialogue. In fact, the Holy Father goes beyond mere ecumenical dialogue to include all dialogue in which the Church presently engages with the purpose of bringing about true reconciliation among people. With his typical clarity of thought, the Holy Father teaches:

> It should be repeated that, on the part of the Church and her members, dialogue, whatever form it takes (and these forms can be and are very diverse, since the very concept of dialogue has an analogical value) can never begin from an attitude of indifference to the truth. On the contrary, it must begin from a presentation of the truth, offered in a calm way, with respect for the intelligence and consciences of others. The dialogue of reconciliation can never replace or attenuate the proclamation of the truth of the Gospel, the precise goal of which is conversion from sin and communion with Christ and the Church. It must be at the service of the transmission and realization of that truth through the means left by Christ to the Church for the pastoral activity of reconciliation, namely catechesis and penance.

This teaching solidly places ecumenical dialogue within the Church's theological and doctrinal Tradition. First of all, Pope

John Paul II addresses the concern that ecumenical dialogue is being used to propagate religious indifferentism. He reiterates that dialogue "can never begin from an attitude of indifference to the truth." He reminds Christians never to approach ecumenical dialogue with an indifference towards the truth. In this way the Holy Father authoritatively closes the door to the possible false usage, or abuse, of ecumenical dialogue. He then reiterates the Second Vatican Council's Catholic principles governing the Church's involvement in ecumenical dialogue. He explains that all dialogue in which the Church is engaged, including that with our separated brethren, "must begin from a presentation of truth."

Vatican II Asserts the Papacy's Traditional Role

Yet what is truth as presented by the Catholic Church? What are the principles with which the Church approaches separated Christians? These are important questions because the schismatic traditionalists or their sympathizers will often argue that in order to facilitate ecumenical dialogue, the Second Vatican Council downplayed the Church's unique claim to be founded by Christ upon the rock of St. Peter. The Council Fathers anticipate these objections in their Declaration on Ecumenism, *Unitatis Redintegratio*. Within this conciliar document, the Council Fathers clearly teach:

> In order to establish this holy Church of His everywhere in the world until the end of time, Christ entrusted to the college of the twelve the task of teaching, ruling, and sanctifying (Cf. Matt. 28:18-20 in conjunction with John 20:21-23). Among their number He chose Peter. After Peter's profession of faith, He decreed that on him He would build His Church; to Peter He promised the keys of the

kingdom of heaven (Cf. Matt. 16:19, in conjunction with Mark 18:18). After Peter's profession of love, Christ entrusted all His sheep to him to be confirmed in faith (Cf. Luke 22:32) and shepherded in perfect unity (Cf. John 21:15-17).

Based on Scriptural foundations, the Second Vatican Council's ecumenical principles flow from the teachings of Christ and His apostles. The Council teaches that our Lord's Church, and hence Christian unity, must be built upon the rock of St. Peter. Furthermore, the Council asserts that the task of preserving and confirming this unity within our Lord's Church rests with St. Peter and his lawful successors within the Roman papacy. The objection that the Second Vatican Council's teachings on ecumenism water down the role of the papacy fails, for this text reiterates what the Church has always taught according to her Sacred Tradition. St. Peter is, and always has been, the foundation of unity among Christians.

Authentic Ecumenism Upholds the Real Presence of Christ in the Eucharist

St. Peter and his successors are the foundation of unity in the Church. However, this foundation is laid down by Jesus Christ. Our Lord is the source of unity within the Church, especially as it concerns His Real Presence in the Most Blessed Sacrament. We should keep this in mind when defending the Council's teachings on ecumenism, since many extreme traditionalists also allege that ecumenism undermines Catholic faith in our Lord's Real Presence in order to appease non-Catholics. This allegation is false. Continue reading Vatican II's decree on ecumenism, and you discover the following teaching: "In His Church [Christ] instituted the wonderful sacrament of the

Eucharist by which the unity of the Church is both signified and brought about."[75]

In other words, the Second Vatican Council calls the Church to promote Christian unity through ecumenical dialogue. Yet the Council recognizes that unity can be neither fully realized nor fully symbolized except through the sacrament of the Holy Eucharist. The Second Vatican Council not only upholds the traditional Catholic position concerning the Most Blessed Sacrament, but the Council clearly states this position in the very decree through which ecumenism is promoted. The Council Fathers, by promoting ecumenical dialogue, seek to bring our separated Christian brethren back to full communion with the Catholic Church by means of the Holy Eucharist. The Eucharist symbolizes our unity within the Church as Catholics, first with God and secondly with each other. Yet this symbolism may only be fully realized through the holy Sacrifice of the Mass.

In bringing to us the Body, Blood, Soul, and Divinity of our Lord Jesus Christ, as well as in perpetuating Christ's holy sacrifice upon the cross, the Mass unites all of Christ's disciples throughout time and space, gathering them into one Church. The intention of the Second Vatican Council's teaching on ecumenism is to help reunite with the Church those Christian disciples who have become separated through historic schisms and heresies.

"This ecumenical position represents a departure from Catholic Tradition," allege many adherents to various traditionalist schisms. "We find no example of the Catholic Church engaging in similar ecumenical activity before Vatican II." This allegation might trouble Catholics, because they are unaware of other examples of the Catholic Church's practice of ecumenism with those who have separated from her. Yet such

precedents do exist within Catholic Tradition. The most striking example is probably the ecumenical Council of Florence.
This entire council offers a clear precedent from Catholic Tradition for the Church's present involvement in ecumenical dialogue. After all, the Council of Florence sought to reunite the
Orthodox East and the Catholic West. During this council's
fourth session, Pope Eugene the IV decreed:

> Eugenius, bishop, servant of the servants of God, for an
> everlasting record. It befits us to render thanks to almighty
> God ... For behold, the western and eastern peoples, who
> have been separated for long, hasten to enter into a pact of
> harmony and unity; and those who were justly distressed at
> the long dissension that kept them apart, at last after many
> centuries, under the impulse of Him from whom every good
> gift comes, meet together in person in this place out of
> desire for holy union.

A couple of matters should draw our attention here. First,
the East and West were obviously separated from one another
in schism, as recognized by Pope Eugene IV in this decree.
These Churches nevertheless came together after many centuries to try to reconcile their differences. This is an act of ecumenism, one that Pope Eugene IV attributes to the Holy Spirit.
In fact, the Pope not only attributes this ecumenical dialogue
to the Holy Spirit's inspiration, but he proceeds to uphold such
dialogue at the Council of Florence as our Christian obligation,
stating: "We are aware that it is our duty and the duty of the
whole Church to strain every nerve to ensure that these happy
initiatives make progress and have issue through our common
care, so that we may deserve to be and to be called co-opera-
tors with God."

Some critics of the Second Vatican Council maintain that this teaching from the Council of Florence applies solely to ecumenical dialogue, not joint prayer between Catholics and non-Catholics. Yet if we re-read the above citation from the Council of Florence, we find that the Pope insists: "It befits *us* to render thanks to almighty God." This is a prayer of thanksgiving to God. Although they had not yet healed their schism, the Roman Pontiff led the Council Fathers gathered from the Catholic West and the Orthodox East in the recitation of this prayer. This is a clear example from Catholic Tradition of a Pope and Catholic bishops praying with those Christian brethren who have been separated from full communion.

Some adherents to post-Vatican II extreme traditionalist schisms disdain the respect shown by the Church towards the ecclesiastical leadership of non-Catholic Churches and denominations. These folks maintain that the Church should continue denouncing non-Catholic spiritual leaders as heretics and schismatics. In departing from the Church's spiritual unity, they claim, Protestant ministers and Orthodox clergy forfeit any spiritual authority they might otherwise possess, and thus any right to be held in respect by the Catholic faithful. This is not the position, however, of Pope Eugene the IV, who said this at the Council of Florence:

> Finally, our most dear son John Palaeologus, emperor of the Romans, together with our venerable brother Joseph, Patriarch of Constantinople, the apocrisiaries of the other patriarchal sees, and a great multitude of archbishops, ecclesiastics, and nobles arrived at their last port, Venice, on 8 February last.

This is recognition, from both Pope Eugene and the Council Fathers, of the religious title and dignity of the Orthodox Emperor John Palaeologus and the Orthodox Patriarch Joseph of Constantinople. Despite his separation from Rome, Patriarch Joseph is welcomed to the Council of Florence by Pope Eugene the IV as a "brother." The Second Vatican Council's approach to ecumenism, by which the Church treats non-Catholic spiritual authorities with both respect and dignity, thus maintains the same ecumenical principles as those upheld at the Council of Florence. No doubt the reality of heresy and schism still exists after the Second Vatican Council (see Canon 751), just as it did before the Council of Florence. However, in dialogue with our separated brethren, the Church chooses not to wave the terms "heretic" and "schismatic" in their faces.

In arguing a traditional Catholic position from the Council of Florence — in other words, a position truly based upon the Church's Sacred Tradition — a Catholic may encounter the objection that these texts apply only to Catholic ecumenism with the Eastern Orthodox. What about Catholic-Protestant ecumenism since the Second Vatican Council? Is there a similar example from previous ecumenical councils?

These are important questions, since many traditionalists often make a big deal over the invitation extended to six Protestant theologians to participate at the Second Vatican Council in an advisory capacity. As a quick aside, we should note that there were many additional Orthodox and Protestant observers at the Council. The famous "six Protestants" constantly flouted by opponents of the Second Vatican Council were simply observers at the Council, which was involved with liturgical reform.

The suggestion that these "six Protestants" virtually put together the reformed Liturgy of Pope Paul VI is a great exaggeration! If we accept the Council of Trent as an authentic expression of Catholic Tradition (as Catholics are obliged to do), then such objections fail to take into account Catholic Tradition. For in the documents of Trent's thirteenth session, we read:

> The sacred and holy general Synod of Trent, lawfully assembled in the Holy Ghost ... grants, as far as regards the holy Synod itself, to all [Protestants] and each one throughout the whole of Germany, whether ecclesiastics or seculars, of whatsoever degree, estate, condition, quality they be, who may wish to repair to this ecumenical and general Council the public faith and full security, which they call a safe-conduct ... so as that they may and shall have it in their power in all liberty to confer, make proposals, and treat on those things which are to be treated of in the said Synod; to come freely and safely to the said ecumenical Council, and there remain and abide, and propose therein, as well in writing as by word of mouth, as many articles as to them shall seem good, and to confer and dispute, without any abuse or contumely, with the fathers, or with those who may have been selected by the said holy Synod; as also to withdraw whensoever they shall think fit.

We should make several important observations here. First, the Council of Trent both invited and offered safe passage to Protestants who wished to come and participate at this ecumenical council. Second, the Council Fathers invited Protestants of all social and ecclesiastical ranks to share their theological views, propose topics for debate, and generally participate in the daily affairs of this ecumenical council. Third, the Council Fathers allowed Protestants to withdraw at any time. Finally, the Council Fathers invited Protestants to be more than simply observers.

At the Council of Trent, the Church clearly issued an invitation to ecumenical dialogue between Catholics and Protestants. And since Lutheranism enveloped most of Germany around the time of the Council, this invitation was much broader than the invitation extended to a handful of Protestant theologians at Vatican II. In fact, the Council of Trent permitted the Protestants attending the Council a *greater* level of participation than was allowed to the Protestant theologians observing Vatican II. Ironically, the Lefebvrite objections to Catholic-Protestant ecumenism, both during and after the Second Vatican Council, are really objections to a precedent set by the *Council of Trent*.

In concluding this chapter on the Second Vatican Council and ecumenism, we can affirm that these teachings offer us a fresh insight into our Catholic Tradition, in that the conciliar fathers formulated these teachings to address the scandal of Christian disunity. Yet when it comes to the substance of our Catholic Faith, these teachings mark no departure from what the Church has always taught. Catholic ecumenism is solidly founded in Catholic Tradition, as handed down from previous ecumenical councils. The teachings of Vatican II on ecumenism build upon the Church's ecumenical precedents established at the Council of Florence and the Council of Trent. As Catholics, we can embrace the Second Vatican Council's teachings on ecumenism, because these teachings are solidly rooted in Catholic Tradition.

PART THREE

A.

Brief Answers to Some
Extreme Traditionalist
Arguments

CHAPTER NINE

Was the Tridentine Liturgy for All Time?

The "Pope St. Pius V and Quo Primum Tempore*" Argument*

One of the first arguments one encounters from SSPX apologists is the *Quo Primum* argument. This argument takes its name from Pope St. Pius V's sixteenth-century papal bull *Quo Primum Tempore*. Many SSPX proponents claim that St. Pius V promulgated the Tridentine Mass in perpetuity, meaning for all time. They argue that every priest has the right to use the Roman Missal codified by St. Pius V in *Quo Primum Tempore*, and that this right cannot be taken away from a priest.

The main problem with the *Quo Primum Tempore* argument is its failure to take into account canonical Tradition. First, this argument does not distinguish between the doctrine and the discipline of the Catholic Church. Yet that distinction is critical.

Briefly put, a dogma is a doctrine the Church formally defines, declaring it with certitude to be infallible. Take, for example, the dogma of the Blessed Mother's assumption into heaven. Pope Pius XII didn't suddenly declare it as a new truth in 1950 that Mary was assumed into heaven; this truth, after all, had come into existence nearly two millennia before when Mary was assumed. Rather, the Holy Father declared this dogma because the Church knew for certain that Mary had been assumed into heaven. At that point, Our Lady's assumption was thus no longer a matter of theological speculation for Catholics. Once declared, a dogma must be believed by the Catholic faithful, and cannot be rejected or abandoned — although the Church may always clarify her understanding of a dogma.

A mere discipline of the Faith, on the other hand, is a law, a custom, or a practice originating from the Church as a means of safeguarding the good order of the Church. To establish ecclesiastical discipline, the Church must ask herself: What is the most practical way of protecting the doctrine of the Church here and now?

Consequently, discipline is subject to change depending upon the present needs of the Church. Furthermore, mere disciplines of the Faith need not be applied in the same manner throughout the entire Church, and they may always be dispensed from, since the pastoral needs of one particular grouping of the faithful may differ from the pastoral needs of another. For example, the discipline of celibacy is imposed upon Catholic priests in the Latin Church, whereas this discipline is optional for Catholic priests in the Eastern Catholic Churches.

Through this insight one sees the weakness of the claim put forward by many SSPX apologists. Within the very text of *Quo Primum Tempore* stands a clause by St. Pius V granting an exception to the declaration: All priests and bishops who said Mass using liturgical missals more than two hundred years old were not obliged to use this codified version of the Roman

Missal. So even from the beginning of its promulgation, *Quo Primum Tempore* never applied to every Catholic priest.

From this fact alone, one can safely draw the correct conclusion that *Quo Primum Tempore* is merely disciplinary. For a dogmatic definition, by its very nature, binds the entire Church, while *Quo Primum Tempore* contains exceptions among the Catholic faithful in its application. Since "equals have no power over one another," as the old canonical principle states, any disciplinary document can be legally changed or revoked by a successor of the one who first promulgated it.

Yet even if this were not the case, and future Roman Pontiffs were forbidden from reforming the Missal codified by St. Pius V, one cannot deny that this papal bull merely granted the right to celebrate Mass according to the Tridentine Missal. *Quo Primum Tempore* did not extend the right to bishops — upon their own authority and against the expressed wishes of the Roman Pontiff — to ordain priests and consecrate bishops as Archbishop Lefebvre had done. In other words, using a certain liturgical Missal to offer the holy Sacrifice of the Mass is not the same action as consecrating bishops without permission of the Roman Pontiff, even if one consecrates bishops in order to provide a source of ordination for priests who will say the Tridentine Liturgy.

CHAPTER TEN

Is the New Mass a "Danger to the Faith"?

The "Novus Ordo Missae *Is Intrinsically Evil*" *Argument*

A common argument now put forward by the SSPX is that the revised Liturgy of Pope Paul VI is intrinsically evil, or at the least poses a proximate danger to the Catholic faith. This would mean that the post-Vatican II Liturgy is in and of itself contrary to the law of God. How individual Lefebvrites approach this issue will often vary, but they typically insist that the new Mass contains heresy, blasphemy, or ambiguity. Interestingly enough, the same text from Catholic Tradition that many schismatic traditionalists quote in support of their claim, when carefully read, actually refutes this very claim.

A preliminary observation is in order. The Mass has not changed since Christ instituted this sacrament on the night before His crucifixion. In essence, there is neither an "old" Mass nor a "new" Mass, but only the Mass. What changed after the Second Vatican Council was not the Mass, but the Liturgy.

This means that while the "accidents" (to use a classical theological term) differ somewhat between the pre-Vatican II Liturgy and the reformed Liturgy of Pope Paul VI, their essence remains the same: the Body, Blood, Soul, and Divinity of Jesus Christ transubstantiated into the Eucharist. This central mystery of the Mass takes place regardless of whether the priest celebrates according to the liturgical books in use before the Second Vatican Council or according to the liturgical books revised by Pope Paul VI. In fact, both sets of liturgical books are usages of the same Roman liturgical rite.

In accusing the reformed Liturgy of being intrinsically evil, many extreme traditionalists quote the seventh canon on the Sacrifice of the Mass from the Council of Trent. This canon states: "If anyone says that the ceremonies, vestments, and outward signs which the Catholic Church makes use of in the celebration of Masses are incentives to impiety, rather than offices of piety; let him be anathema."

Let's look at this more closely. Since the definition of intrinsic evil is "something which in and of itself is evil," we see from the Council of Trent that an approved Liturgy of the Church cannot be evil. For something that is intrinsically evil is naturally an incentive to impiety, while the Council of Trent declares dogmatically that the approved liturgical ceremonies of the Catholic Church cannot be incentives to impiety.

Is the revised Liturgy of Pope Paul VI an approved Liturgy of the Church? Of course it is! So according to the Tradition of the Church as dogmatically defined at the Ecumenical Council of Trent, one can only conclude that the reformed Liturgy of Pope Paul VI cannot be an incentive to impiety. It necessarily follows, then, that neither could it be intrinsically evil.

CHAPTER ELEVEN

Is Consecrating a Bishop Merely an "Act of Disobedience"?

The "Illicit Consecration of Bishops Is Not an Act of Schism" Argument

One argument commonly presented within SSPX circles is that the act of consecrating bishops without papal permission is an act of disobedience, but not an act of schism. The SSPX folks generally claim that they have not withdrawn subjection to the Roman Pontiff. Rather, they refuse obedience in some matters.

We should reiterate here that Canon 752 defines schism as "the withdrawal of submission to the Supreme Pontiff or from communion with the members of the Church subject to him." Notice that the canon does not distinguish between degrees of withdrawal of submission to the Roman Pontiff. In other words, a person need not completely withdraw submission to the Roman Pontiff to enter into a state of schism. Rather, partial withdrawal of obedience in certain matters — and consecrating bishops without papal mandate is a serious matter —

remains an act through which a person withdraws submission to the Roman Pontiff. In short, the Holy Father told Archbishop Lefebvre not to consecrate bishops without Rome's permission, and Archbishop Lefebvre refused to submit.

In so doing, Arcbishop Lefebvre and the four men he illicitly ordained as bishops plunged themselves headlong into schism. Which means that, once again, this SSPX argument is empty and futile.

CHAPTER TWELVE

A Heretic Pope?

The "Pope Liberius" Argument

Probably the most common claim one comes across within circles sympathetic to the SSPX is that Pope Liberius (reigned A.D. 352-366), fearful of the Arian heretics, falsely excommunicated St. Athanasius. Some even accuse Pope Liberius of giving in to the Arian heresy. For this reason, the SSPX claims, Pope Liberius became the first Pope in the history of the Church not to be recognized as a saint. By analogy the SSPX considers Archbishop Lefebvre a modern St. Athanasius and Pope John Paul II a modern Pope Liberius.

Their argument is that if it happened once, it can happen again. And yet, Catholic Tradition paints a slightly different picture. For example, Henri Denzinger's *Sources of Catholic Dogma* lists Pope Liberius as "St. Liberius." Similarly, St. Jerome includes Liberius in his martyrology.[76]

Additionally, one finds in Denzinger a copy of the papal epistle authored by Pope St. Anastasius subtitled "The Orthodoxy of Pope Liberius." In it, Pope St. Anastasius clearly states:

The heretical African faction [of the Arian heresy] was not able by any deception to introduce its baseness because, as we believe, our God provided that that holy and untarnished faith be not contaminated through any vicious blasphemy of slanderous men — that faith which had been discussed and defended at the meeting of the synod of Nicea by the holy men and bishops now placed in the resting place of the saints (Art. 93 of the Thirtieth Edition).

Who were these holy men and how does this relate to Pope Liberius? Well, Pope St. Anastasius answers these questions in the subsequent paragraph: "For this faith, those who were then esteemed as holy bishops gladly endured exile, that is ... Liberius, bishop of the Roman Church."

Should one believe the SSPX Archbishop Lefebvre concerning Liberius? Or should one believe the claim of Anastasius — one who was a saint, a Pope, and a writer much closer to the time the Arian heresy took place?

CHAPTER THIRTEEN

Are There Now "Two Romes"?

The "Traditional Rome vs. Modernist Rome" Argument

The question of Rome eventually weighs upon the conscience of anyone who leaves the Church. Given what Catholic Tradition consistently teaches concerning faithfulness to Rome, how can one claim to be traditional Catholic and justify separation from the Roman Pontiff?

The SSPX offer a novel answer to this question. Many claim that the behavior of the post-Vatican II Popes has divided the faithful into two camps. One camp, the institutional Church, is faithful to contemporary Rome, which Archbishop Lefebvre claims has been infiltrated by modernists and liberals. The other camp contains those such as the SSPX, who naturally are faithful to Traditional Rome.

Let us examine what Pope Pius XII says within his papal encyclical *Mystici Corporis*:

> We think how grievously they err who arbitrarily claim that
> the Church is something hidden and invisible, as they also

do who look upon her as a mere human institution possessing a certain disciplinary code and external ritual, but
lacking power to communicate supernatural life (Par. 64).

This theological insight establishes, from the Church's Tradition, that one cannot separate the Church into a mere spiritual communion or a mere human institution. In short, the
Rome of Tradition and the Rome of today are the same Rome.
Just as at the Incarnation Christ was fully human and fully
divine, without sacrificing either nature, so too must the
Church, as Christ's mystical body, be a perfect union of the visible and the invisible.

As St. Paul asks, "Is Christ divided?" (1 Corinthians 1:13).
Of course, the answer remains no. Therefore, how can one
divide Christ's mystical body into a mere spiritual communion or a mere human one?

Mystici Corporis continues:

> But we must not think that He rules only in a hidden or
> extraordinary manner. On the contrary, our Redeemer also
> governs His mystical body in a visible and normal way
> through His vicar on earth … Since He was all-wise, He
> could not leave the body of the Church He had founded as
> a human society without a visible head … That Christ and
> His vicar constitute the one and only Head is the solemn
> teaching of our predecessor of immortal memory, Boniface
> VIII, in the apostolic letter *Unam Sanctam*; and his succes-
> sors have never ceased to repeat the same. (Par. 40)

The Roman Pontiff and Jesus Christ form but one head of
the Catholic Church. The word "tradition" comes from the
Latin verb *tradere*, which means "to hand down." Ultimately,

there must be a source from which Tradition was first passed down, and that source is Jesus Christ. As Christ and His vicar constitute but one Head of the Church, then the voice of Tradition must speak through St. Peter and his lawful successors in the Roman primacy. Therefore, to follow Tradition one must embrace today's successor to the rock upon whom Christ founded His mystical body.

In the end, our liturgical tradition as Catholics cannot be preserved apart from Pope John Paul II and his predecessors, all the other legitimate successors of St. Peter. For his voice is the voice of Catholic Tradition in the Church today — a Tradition that has been passed down to him by Christ and the apostles.

PART THREE

B.

The Church Does Not
Abandon Her Sheep

CHAPTER FOURTEEN

Faithful Alternatives for Traditionalists

∽

THE CLASSICAL ROMAN LITURGY is one of the Church's greatest treasures. Thus all our efforts to preserve the Tridentine Liturgy must take place in full union with the Holy Father and the diocesan bishop.

— LOIC MERIAN, FOUNDER OF CIEL

Are all traditionalists schismatic? The answer is no. In fact, one of the present authors (Pete Vere) continues to frequent the old Latin Liturgy on a regular basis and he remains firmly committed to its preservation. There are indeed several traditionalist apostolates operating in full communion with Rome. To find out if any such legitimate traditionalist alternatives operate in one's diocese, one need only contact the local chancery office. Below are short descriptions of five of the more popular traditionalist alternatives recognized by the Church.

The Priestly Fraternity of St. Peter

The Priestly Fraternity of St. Peter (FSSP), often referred to within traditionalist circles simply as "the Fraternity," began with several priests and seminarians who left the SSPX in 1988 because they could not in good conscience go along with Archbishop Lefebvre's schismatic consecration of bishops. Pope John Paul II brought together a group of these men who wished to continue celebrating the sacraments according to the traditionalist Liturgy while remaining in full communion with the Church and founded the FSSP as a society of apostolic life. Its purpose is to minister the sacraments according to the liturgical books in use in 1962. Additionally, the FSSP serves as a point of reception for former SSPX clergy seeking to reconcile with the Church.

From its initial founding of under a dozen priests and seminarians, the FSSP now boasts over a hundred priests, almost as many seminarians, apostolates on every continent, and several schools — including two international seminaries. The FSSP's current superior general is Fr. Arnaud Devillers — a French priest originally ordained by Archbishop Lefebvre for the SSPX. Father Devillers reconciled with the Church about a year after Lefebvre's schismatic consecration of bishops. Father Devillers is a formidable administrator as well as a keen visionary within the FSSP. During his tenure as District Superior for the FSSP in America, he oversaw the FSSP's expansion into Canada and Australia, as well as the founding and initial construction of the FSSP's English-speaking seminary. As superior general of the FSSP, Father has brought his keen sense of ecclesiology to the job — leading traditionalists who wish to remain faithful to Rome into the Church's mainstream, while dispelling numerous negative misconceptions about traditionalists formerly held by many within the Church hierarchy.

The Apostolic Administration of St. John Vianney

When Archbishop Lefebvre consecrated four bishops without a papal mandate in 1988, he did not act alone. Rather, accompanying him to the altar as co-consecrator was his old friend Bishop Antonio Castro de Mayer — the retired bishop of Campos, Brazil. Previously, Bishop Castro de Mayer had founded the Priestly Union of St. John Vianney as a sort of traditionalist shadow-diocese from among many of his former diocesan priests in Campos, Brazil. In the years immediately following the schism, these priests and seminarians interacted extensively with those of the SSPX. When Bishop Castro de Mayer passed away, the SSPX illicitly consecrated one of Bishop Castro de Mayer's priests to the episcopate. Msgr. Lionel Rangel thus became the fifth bishop in Archbishop Lefebvre's illicit episcopal lineage.

During the Great Jubilee of the year 2000, relations between the SSPX and the Holy See softened enough to initiate serious negotiations. Subsequently, the Priestly Union of St. John Vianney was invited to join the SSPX in the negotiations. Due to failing health, however, Bishop Rangel could not be present in Rome for the negotiations. So he asked his vicar general, Msgr. Rifan, to attend the discussion in Rome on his behalf.

Over the next year, the negotiations between the SSPX proved rather stormy as the SSPX continued to make ever greater demands. In contrast, Rome's negotiations with Msgr. Rifan went well as he kept the demands of the Priestly Union modest. When the discussion between the Holy See and the SSPX collapsed altogether, Bishop Rangel faced a great dilemma — should he instruct his vicar general to continue the discussion with Rome, or should he pull back in order to avoid breaking ranks with the SSPX. After much prayer and reflection, he chose the former.

Not only did God allow Bishop Rangel to become the first bishop in Lefebvre's illicit episcopal lineage to reconcile with the Church, but the bishop also saw Rome erect the Priestly Union he led into the Apostolic Administration of St. John

Vianney — a near diocesan structure. Bishop Rangel was recognized as bishop of his people and Rome gave him the same pastoral authority over the traditionalist priests and laity of Campos as a diocesan bishop.

Yet Bishop Rangel's health continued to degenerate and he soon found himself thinking of a successor. As vicar general, Msgr. Rifan had proven himself a faithful son of the good bishop throughout the negotiations. The vicar general had also impressed Rome with his humility during the same negotiations, while endearing himself to his fellow traditionalists — both priests and laity — back home in Campos. Thus everyone agreed Msgr. Rifan was the best candidate to succeed Bishop Rangel as apostolic administrator of the Campos traditionalists. Shortly before God called him to Himself, Bishop Rangel accepted the Holy See's invitation to participate in the consecration to the episcopacy of his successor. Thus Msgr. Rifan became the first bishop consecrated for traditionalist apostolate since the introduction of Pope Paul VI's liturgical reform.

Today, under the successful leadership of Bishop Rifan, the Apostolic Administration boasts over thirty-five priests, thirty-thousand laity, a seminary, and dozens of parishes. Its territory is parallel to that of the Diocese of Campos, and where the competent bishop of another diocese permits, priests of the Apostolic Administration of St. John Vianney may serve traditionalists located in other dioceses as well. Additionally, Bishop Rifan serves as an unofficial ambassador throughout the Church for traditionalists who have chosen to remain in full communion with Rome.

Centre International d'Etudes Liturgique

Although often mistaken for ICEL, the Centre International d'Etudes Liturgique (a.k.a. CIEL) is firmly committed to promoting the traditional Latin Liturgy. Not only is CIEL a completely lay-run organization, but it approaches the classical Roman Liturgy uniquely from a scholarly and non-polemic perspective. Thus its research is well-respected by many scholars, seminaries, pontifical faculties, bishops and cardinals from around the world — the majority of whom are not traditionalist per se, but who recognize CIEL's work as a valuable contribution to liturgical dialogue.

CIEL boasts delegates from over forty nations, and each year hosts an international colloquium on the traditional Roman Liturgy. Gathering in France where CIEL was founded, some of the most respected liturgists, scholars of the sacred sciences, and members of the Church hierarchy present papers covering particular aspects of classical Liturgy. These colloquiums are open to all those interested in Catholic Liturgy, and not merely traditionalists. The proceedings from the colloquium are subsequently translated into several languages and then published.

Speaking of CIEL's contribution to the wider liturgical dialogue within the Church, Shawn Tribe, CIEL's Canadian delegate, writes:

> We stress the importance of unity in legitimate diversity. Thus, you find that, while the focus of CIEL and CIEL-Canada is squarely upon the academic study of the classical Roman Liturgy, CIEL-Canada realizes that this charism does not exclude other liturgical initiatives consistent with or part of the Catholic liturgical tradition.

The Catholic Church has always been composed of a variety of liturgical rites. Hence, CIEL-Canada finds itself to be allied in a spirit of fraternity to all who have a profound love and reverence for the Church, her teachings, and her liturgies. This includes not only those who have a love for the Roman Liturgy according to the 1962 *Missale Romanum*, but also those of the various Byzantine and Oriental rites (who are obviously in an especially venerable category given the richness, antiquity, and venerability of their liturgical rites — not to mention theology, ecclesiology, and spirituality), of the Anglican use in the Latin Rite, and of those who seek the celebration or reform of the 1970 *Roman Missal* in accordance with the true spirit and letter of the Second Vatican Council and *Sacrosanctum Concilium* — as enunciated by the magisterial authority of the Church. In the latter group we find many laudable societies and organizations, such as *Adoremus* and the Reform of the Reform liturgical school of thought.

These are all a part of the "multiple treasures of Catholicism," of that "beauty and unity in variety" and of that legitimate diversity which has always been found in the one, holy, catholic, and apostolic Church. Thus it is clear that the work of CIEL is of broad interest and relevance, for it has diverse applications to the many legitimate liturgical initiatives out there.

The Benedictine Monastery of St. Madeleine de Le Barroux

In the early 1970's, a young Benedictine monk named Dom Gérard Calvet set out to restore the abandoned monastery of St. Madeleine de Le Barroux in France. Because he sought to live by the pre-Vatican II Benedictine discipline, he could not find anyone within the Church hierarchy to ordain the young men who joined him in this endeavor. Dom Gérard then turned to Archbishop Lefebvre, and the two became close friends. For years their respective communities worked closely together within the traditionalist movement.

Nevertheless, Dom Gérard could not bring himself in good conscience to support Lefebvre's illicit consecration of bishops. Thus, shortly after Lefebvre went into schism in 1988, Dom Gérard sought reconciliation with Rome on behalf of his monastery. Not only did the Holy See regularize the canonical situation of him and his monks, but within a few years Le Barroux monastery was raised to the status of abbey, welcomed into the Benedictine federation, and Dom Gérard consecrated its abbot. Today, St. Madeleine de Le Barroux monastery boasts well over a hundred monks, a sister monastery for cloistered nuns, and arguably the leading theologian among traditionalists in full communion with Rome, namely, Dom Basile Valuet, O.S.B.

Diocesan *Ecclesia Dei* Indult Mass Centers

The number of traditionalist religious orders and institutes of consecrated life operating in full communion with Rome now surpasses two dozen. Yet diocesan priests still offer the bulk of traditional Latin Liturgies celebrated in full communion with Rome. In 1984, after years of suppression, Pope John Paul II gave the bishops of the world permission to allow for the celebration of the Mass according to the 1962 Liturgy. Canonists refer to this allowance as an indult, meaning a relaxation of the law that requires priests of the Latin Church to celebrate the sacraments according to the liturgical reform of Pope Paul VI. Nevertheless, several restrictions were placed upon the 1984 indult. Additionally, bishops who granted an indult in their diocese were required to file an inordinate amount of extra paperwork each year. As a result, the number of indults granted for the celebration of the traditional Liturgy of the Mass remained minimal.

This changed in 1988 when Pope John Paul II promulgated *Ecclesia Dei* in response to Archbishop Lefebvre's schism. In calling for "a wide and generous"[77] application of the *Ecclesia Dei* indult, the Holy Father lifted most of the previous restrictions placed upon the traditional Liturgy and eliminated the extra paperwork involved. He also extended permission for diocesan bishops to allow for the other sacraments to be celebrated according to the liturgical books used in 1962. Basically, Rome took a hands-off approach — allowing each diocesan bishop to determine the level of pastoral support for traditionalists within his respective diocese.

Thus the celebration of the sacraments according to the *Ecclesia Dei* indult differs in each diocese where it is implemented. Some bishops only see the need for the celebration of Mass according to the traditional Liturgy once a month in their diocese and do not allow for the celebration of any other sacrament. Others, however, have reserved a parish in their diocese exclusively for the daily celebration of the sacraments according to the traditional Liturgy, and even perform ordinations when a suitable traditionalist candidate is presented.

Conclusion — An Invitation

The authors, who themselves are traditionalists who love and revere the ancient liturgical patrimony of the Church, respectfully encourage all Catholics, especially traditionalist Catholics, to avail themselves of any and all lawful opportunities, such as those mentioned above, to maintain and deepen their love for Catholic Tradition.

APPENDICES

Apostolic Letter "Ecclesia Dei" of the Supreme Pontiff John Paul II Given *Motu Proprio*

1. With great affliction the Church has learned of the unlawful episcopal ordination conferred on 30 June last by Archbishop Marcel Lefebvre, which has frustrated all the efforts made during the previous years to ensure the full communion with the Church of the Priestly Fraternity of St. Pius X founded by the same Msgr. Lefebvre. These efforts, especially intense during recent months, in which the Apostolic See has shown comprehension to the limits of the possible, were all to no avail.(1)

2. This affliction was particularly felt by the Successor Peter to whom in the first place pertains the guardianship of the unity of the Church,(2) even though the number of persons directly involved in these events might be few. For

every person is loved by God on his own account and has been redeemed by the blood of Christ shed on the Cross for the salvation of all.

The particular circumstances, both objective and subjective, in which Archbishop Lefebvre acted, provide everyone with an occasion for profound reflection and for a renewed pledge of fidelity to Christ and to His Church.

3. In itself, this act was one of *disobedience* to the Roman Pontiff in a very grave matter and of supreme importance for the unity of the Church, such as is the ordination of bishops whereby the apostolic succession is sacramentally perpetuated. Hence such disobedience — which implies in practice the rejection of the Roman primacy — constitutes a *schismatic* act.(3) In performing such an act, notwithstanding the formal *canonical warning* sent to them by the cardinal prefect of the Congregation for Bishops on 17 June last, Msgr. Lefebvre and the priests Bernard Fellay, Bernard Tissier de Mallerais, Richard Williamson, and Alfonso de Galarreta, have incurred the grave penalty of excommunication envisaged by ecclesiastical law.(4)

4. The *root* of this schismatic act can be discerned in an incomplete and contradictory notion of Tradition. Incomplete, because it does not take sufficiently into account the *living* character of Tradition, which, as the Second Vatican Council clearly taught, "comes from the apostles and progresses in the Church with the help of the Holy Spirit. There is a growth in insight into the realities and words that are being passed on. This comes about in various ways. It comes through the contemplation and study of believers who ponder these things in their hearts. It comes from the intimate sense of spiritual realities which they experience.

And it comes from the preaching of those who have received, along with their right of succession in the episcopate, the sure charism of truth."(5)

But especially contradictory is a notion of Tradition which opposes the universal magisterium of the Church possessed by the Bishop of Rome and the Body of Bishops. It is impossible to remain faithful to the Tradition while breaking the ecclesial bond with him to whom, in the person of the Apostle Peter, Christ himself entrusted the ministry of unity in his Church.(6)

5. Faced with the situation that has arisen, I deem it my duty to inform all the Catholic faithful of some aspects which this sad event has highlighted.

a) The outcome of the movement promoted by Msgr. Lefebvre can and must be, for all the Catholic faithful, a motive for sincere reflection concerning their own fidelity to the Church's Tradition, authentically interpreted by the ecclesiastical magisterium, ordinary and extraordinary, especially in the Ecumenical Councils from Nicaea to Vatican II. From this reflection all should draw a renewed and efficacious conviction of the necessity of strengthening still more their fidelity by rejecting erroneous interpretations and arbitrary and unauthorized applications in matters of doctrine, liturgy, and discipline.

To the bishops especially it pertains, by reason of their pastoral mission, to exercise the important duty of a clear-sighted vigilance full of charity and firmness, so that this fidelity may be everywhere safeguarded.(7)

However, it is necessary that all the pastors and the other faithful have a new awareness, not only of the lawfulness but also of the richness for the Church of a diversity of charisms, traditions of spirituality and apostolate, which also constitutes the beauty of unity in variety: of that blended "harmony" which the earthly Church raises up to heaven under the impulse of the Holy Spirit.

b) Moreover, I should like to remind theologians and other experts in the ecclesiastical sciences that they should feel themselves called upon to answer in the present circumstances. Indeed, the extent and depth of the teaching of the Second Vatican Council call for a renewed commitment to deeper study in order to reveal clearly the Council's continuity with Tradition, especially in points of doctrine which, perhaps because they are new, have not yet been well understood by some sections of the Church.

c) In the present circumstances I wish especially to make an appeal both solemn and heartfelt, paternal and fraternal, to all those who until now have been linked in various ways to the movement of Archbishop Lefebvre, that they may fulfill the grave duty of remaining united to the Vicar of Christ in the unity of the Catholic Church, and of ceasing their support in any way for that movement. Everyone should be aware that formal adherence to the schism is a grave offence against God and carries the penalty of excommunication decreed by the Church's law.(8)

To all those Catholic faithful who feel attached to some previous liturgical and disciplinary forms of the

Latin tradition, I wish to manifest my will to facilitate their ecclesial communion by means of the necessary measures to guarantee respect for their rightful aspirations. In this matter I ask for the support of the bishops and of all those engaged in the pastoral ministry in the Church.

6. Taking account of the importance and complexity of the problems referred to in this document, by virtue of my apostolic authority I decree the following:

a) a *commission* is instituted whose task it will be to collaborate with the bishops, with the departments of the Roman curia and with the circles concerned, for the purpose of facilitating full ecclesial communion of priests, seminarians, religious communities or individuals until now linked in various ways to the Fraternity founded by Msgr. Lefebvre, who may wish to remain united to the Successor Peter in the Catholic Church, while preserving their spiritual and liturgical traditions, in the light of the Protocol signed on 5 May last by Cardinal Ratzinger and Msgr. Lefebvre;

b) this commission is composed of a Cardinal President and other members of the Roman curia, in a number that will be deemed opportune according to circumstances;

c) moreover, respect must everywhere be shown for the feelings of all those who are attached to the Latin liturgical tradition, by a wide and generous application of the directives already issued some time ago by the Apostolic See for the use of the Roman Missal according to the typical edition of 1962.(9)

7. As this year specially dedicated to the Blessed Virgin is now drawing to a close, I wish to exhort all to join in unceasing prayer that the Vicar of Christ, through the intercession of the Mother of the Church, addresses to the Father in the very words of the Son: "That they all may be one!"

Given at Rome, at St. Peter's,
2 July 1988, the tenth year of the pontificate.
JOANNES PAULUS PP. II

Notes:

(1) Cf. "Informatory Note" of 16 June 1988: *L'Osservatore Romano*. English edition, 27 June 1988, pp. 1-2.

(2) Cf. Vatican Council I, Const. *Pastor Aeternus*, cap. 3: *DS* 3060.

(3) Cf. *Code of Canon Law*, Canon 751.

(4) Cf. *Code of Canon Law*, Canon 1382.

(5) Vatican Council II. Const. *Dei Verbum*, No. 8. Cf. Vatican Council I, Const. *Dei Filius*, cap. 4: *DS* 3020.

(6) Cf. Mt. 16:18; Lk. 10:16; Vatican Council I, Const. *Pastor Aeternus*, cap. 3: *DS* 3060.

(7) Cf. *Code of Canon Law*, Canon 386; Paul VI. Apost. Exhort. *Quinque iam anni*, 8 Dec. 1970: *AAS* 63 (1971) pp. 97-106.

(8) Cf. *Code of Canon Law*, Canon 1364.

(9) Cf. Congregation for Divine Worship, Letter *Quattuor abhinc annos*. 3 Oct. 1984: *AAS* 76 (1984) pp. 1088-1089.

APPENDIX II

The Excommunication of Followers of Archbishop Lefebvre

[The following translation and commentary is provided by the Canon Law Society of Great Britain and Ireland (CLSGBI). It is used with the permission of Msgr. Gordon Read and the Canon Law Society of Great Britain and Ireland]

Annexe to Prot. No. 5233/96
Pontifical Council for the Interpretation of Legislative Texts

Note: On the excommunication for schism which the adherents to the movement of Bishop Marcel Lefebvre incur.

1. From the *motu proprio Ecclesia Dei* of July 2, 1988, and from the decree *"Dominus Marcellus Lefebvre"* of the Congregation for Bishops, of July 1, 1988, it appears above all that the schism of Msgr. Lefebvre was declared in immediate reaction to the episcopal ordinations conferred on June 30, 1988, without pontifical mandate (Cf. CIC, Canon 1382). All the same it also appears clear from the aforementioned documents that such a most grave act of disobedience

formed the consummation of a progressive global situation of a schismatic character.

2. In effect, No. 4 of the *motu proprio* explains the nature of the "doctrinal root of this schismatic act," and warns that a "formal adherence to the schism" (by which one must understand "the movement of Archbishop Lefebvre") would bring with it the excommunication established by the universal law of the Church (CIC, Canon 1364, Par. 1). Also, the decree of the Congregation for Bishops makes explicit reference to the "schismatic nature" of the aforesaid episcopal ordinations and mentions the most grave penalty of excommunication which adherence "to the schism of Msgr. Lefebvre" would bring with it.

3. Unfortunately, the schismatic act which gave rise to the *motu proprio* and the decree did no more than draw to a conclusion, in a particularly visible and unequivocal manner — with a most grave formal act of disobedience to the Roman Pontiff — a process of distancing from hierarchical communion. As long as there are no changes which may lead to the re-establishment of this necessary communion, the whole Lefebvrian movement is to be held schismatic, in view of the existence of a formal declaration by the Supreme Authority on this matter.

4. One cannot furnish any judgment on the argumentation of Murray's thesis (see below) because it is not known, and the two articles which refer to it appear confused. However, doubt cannot reasonably be cast upon the validity of the excommunication of the bishops declared in the *motu proprio* and the decree. In particular, it does not seem that one may be able to find, as far as the imputability of the

penalty is concerned, any exempting or lessening circumstances. (Cf. CIC, Canon 1323) As far as the state of necessity in which Msgr. Lefebvre thought to find himself, one must keep before one that such a state must be verified objectively, and there is never a necessity to ordain bishops contrary to the will of the Roman Pontiff, head of the college of bishops. This would, in fact, imply the possibility of "serving" the church by means of an attempt against its unity in an area connected with the very foundations of this unity.

5. As the *motu proprio* declares in No. 5c, the excommunication *latae sententiae* for schism regards those who "adhere formally" to the said schismatic movement. Even if the question of the exact import of the notion of "formal adherence to the schism" would be a matter for the Congregation for the Doctrine of the Faith, it seems to this pontifical council that such formal adherence would have to imply two complementary elements:

a) One of internal nature, consisting in a free and informed agreement with the substance of the schism, in other words, in the choice made in such a way of the followers of Archbishop Lefebvre which puts such an option above obedience to the Pope (at the root of this attitude there will usually be positions contrary to the magisterium of the Church).

b) The other of an external character, consisting in the externalizing of this option, the most manifest sign of which will be the exclusive participation in Lefebvrian "ecclesial" acts, without taking part in the acts of the Catholic Church (one is dealing however with a sign that is not univocal, since there is the possibility that a member of the faithful may take part in the liturgical functions of the followers of Lefebvre but without going along with their schismatic spirit).

6. In the case of the Lefebvrian deacons and priests, there seems no doubt that their ministerial activity in the ambit of the schismatic movement is a more than evident sign of the fact that the two requirements mentioned above (No. 5) are met, and thus that there is a formal adherence.

7. On the other hand, in the case of the rest of the faithful, it is obvious that an occasional participation in liturgical acts or the activity of the Lefebvrian movement, done without making one's own the attitude of doctrinal and disciplinary disunion of such a movement, does not suffice for one to be able to speak of formal adherence to the movement. In pastoral practice, the result can be that it is more difficult to judge their situation. One must take account above all of the person's intentions, and the putting into practice of this internal disposition. For this reason the various situations are going to be judged case by case, in the competent forums both internal and external.

8. All the same, it will always be necessary to distinguish between the moral question on the existence or not of the sin of schism and the juridical-penal question on the existence of the delict of schism, and its consequent sanction. In this latter case the dispositions of Book VI of the *Code of Canon Law* (including Canons 1323-1324) will be applied.

9. It does not seem advisable to make more precise the requirements for the delict of schism (but one would need

to ask the competent dicastery; Cf. Apostolic Constitution *Pastor Bonus*, art. 52). One might risk creating more problems by means of rigid norms of a penal kind which would not cover every case, leaving uncovered cases of substantial schism, or having regard to external behavior which is not always subjectively schismatic.

10. Always from the pastoral point of view it would also seem opportune to recommend once again to sacred pastors all the norms of the *motu proprio Ecclesia Dei* with which the solicitude of the vicar of Christ encouraged to dialogue and has provided the supernatural and human means necessary to facilitate the return of the Lefebvrians to full ecclesial communion.

— VATICAN CITY, AUGUST 24, 1996

Comment:

Although dated August 1996, presumably its publication early in 1998 was in view, at least in part, of the forthcoming tenth anniversary of the consecrations and the issuing of the *motu proprio* and decree.

While initiatives taken under their auspices have had a positive impact, with a number of new religious institutes, and flourishing vocations, now in full communion with the Holy See, and increasingly welcomed by diocesan bishops in some parts of the world, it is also true that there are many places where little attention has been given to its implementation.

Moreover, while the Lefebvrist movement has had some setbacks, the number of adherents has not diminished significantly. A recent book to mark twenty-five years of the Society of St. Pius X in Britain (R. Warwick, *The Living Flame*, London, 1997) indicates that there are some twenty Lefebvrist church buildings in Great Britain at present, with some 2000 regular worshipers. In the United States, the situation is more extensive and much more varied, with many independent priests and chapels, as well as more extremely sedevacantist groups such as the Society of St. Pius V and the Mount St. Michael Community.

The question of apostolic succession has also become more complex. The fissiparous nature of such groups means that not all their orders are derived from Archbishop Lefebvre. Some, having departed from the Society of St. Pius X, have obtained orders or episcopal consecration from Archbishop Ngo Dinh Thuc, or his successors, Bishop Alfred Mendez (formerly of Arecibo), or from Old Catholic and similar sources. For details of the American scene, one should consult M. Cuneo, *The Smoke of Satan*, New York, 1997, a book which is informative if irritatingly discursive.

Supporters of the Society of St. Pius X frequently distribute leaflets containing highly selective or tendentious quotations. One, for example, claims that the society is neither schismatic nor excommunicated. Generally, the line of argument is that since Archbishop Lefebvre was not schismatic, he was not excommunicated, and *a fortiori* neither were any of his followers.

The leaflet quotes Cardinal Castillo Lara to the effect that consecrating a bishop without the Pope's permission is not in itself a schismatic act. It continues that merely to consecrate bishops, without intending to set up an alternative hierarchy in the jurisdictional sense is not an act of schism. Several canonists are quoted as endorsing these views, Count Neri Capponi, an advocate accredited to the Signatura, Professor Geringer of Munich University, Fr. Patrick Valdini, Professor of Canon Law at the Catholic Institute of Paris, and Fr. Gerald Murray, who presented his thesis on the subject at the Gregorian University.

Reference is also made to the decision of the Congregation of the Doctrine of the Faith, dated June 28, 1993, that the excommunication imposed on followers of Archbishop Lefebvre on May 1, 1991, by Bishop Ferraio of Hawaii was invalid since there had been no schismatic acts in the strict sense. One cannot be certain as to the accuracy of such quotations, at least in terms of completeness. For example, the decree mentioned added a rider that there were other grounds on which the bishop could take action.

I am not aware whether Father Murray's thesis has been published, but it would appear that the council had been sent not the thesis but two articles published in the Fall issue of *Latin Mass* magazine. The first was an interview with Father Murray conducted by Roger McCaffrey (pp. 50-55). The second was a summary of the thesis prepared by Steven Terenzio (pp. 55-61).

Murray's first line of argument appears to be that the lay followers of Society of St. Pius X do not incur the excommunication, because only an external violation of a law or precept can be subject to a canonical penalty, and there must be grave imputability. The warnings contained in the *motu proprio* give no specific indications as to what constitutes "adherence," making liability to penalty at least open to doubt.

A second line of argument is that the archbishop denied schism, and that simple disobedience does not constitute schism, only systematic and habitual refusal of dependence.

A third line of argument is that an erroneous view that necessity justified his action would have made his action culpable, but removed canonical malice and therefore liability to excommunication (Canon 1323, No. 7). His argument in effect is that the provisions of the 1983 *Code of Canon Law* are so exigent for imputability to be proved and a penalty incurred that the archbishop and his followers escape by virtue of the very post-conciliar legislation they so oppose:

> On the other hand, Canon 209 prescribes: "Par. 1. Christ's faithful are bound to preserve their communion with the Church at all times, even in their external actions. Par. 2. They are to carry out with great diligence their responsibilities towards both the universal Church and the particular Church to which by law they belong." It is obvious that a lay person who exclusively frequents chapels directed by suspended priests of the Society of St. Pius X, which operate without the permission of either the local or the universal Church, is not, in fact, at the very least, living in external communion with the Church. Thus we have the anomalous situation of a group of faithful who are in fact in some real way living apart from real communion with the Church, but who are almost certainly not subject to the canonical penalties intended to discourage and punish such behavior. (cited from Terenzio, art. cit. p. 61).

The note was clearly prepared as a reply to the arguments of this kind (Cf. No. 4). The suggestion that there might be any doubt cast upon the excommunication declared by the Congregation for Bishops in the case of the archbishop and those he consecrated is given short shrift.

It might be worth remembering that the penalty was raised to excommunication because of the creation of the Patriotic Catholic Association in China, and consecration of bishops without a mandate. The 1917 *Code of Canon Law* (Canon 2370) had provided only for suspension.

Historically, the situation had arisen in Latin America when difficult travel conditions had delayed the arrival of the mandate, and a planned consecration had gone ahead without it, but with no schismatic intent. Here the situation was quite different, and although the intention might not have been to set up an alternative jurisdiction, only to provide for the sacraments, *de facto* that is what was already happening. Moreover, since the protocol originally signed by Archbishop Lefebvre actually provided for the consecration of one bishop, necessity could hardly be argued.

The note then turns to those whose excommunication has not been declared: the clergy and faithful associated with the Society of St. Pius X. The council prescinds from any decision that might be made by the Congregation for the Doctrine of the Faith, but sets out two general legal criteria that would be required for "formal adherence."

The first is an internal criterion, one of intention. An external violation of a law cannot incur a penalty where there is inculpable ignorance, inadvertence, or error with regard to violating the law (Canon 1323, No. 2). Equally the penalty must be reduced where the person was unaware of the penalty, through no fault of their own, or lacked full imputability (Canon 1324, Nos. 9 and 10). There is a requirement of schismatic intention; that is freely and consciously accepting the substance of the schism, putting one's personal choice above obedience to the Pope. Generally, this will be characterized by a habitual stance contrary to the magisterium of the Church.

The second criterion is external, the external effect given to this choice. The most obvious sign of this is to attend solely and exclusively those celebrations conducted by followers of Archbishop Lefebvre, and eschewing those of the mainstream Church, not only local bishop and clergy, but, for example, those legitimately using the 1962 liturgical books, such as the Fraternity of St. Peter.

To a degree the council is accepting the argumentation presented by Father Murray in that an external violation of the law is required, not simply a supposed internal attitude of mind, and that more is required subjectively than attendance even habitually at Lefebvrist centers or celebrations. The latter is compatible with an internal disposition which still accepts the authority of the Pope. However, it parts company with him in that it argues that the disobedience involved in aligning oneself with the Lefebvrists itself implies a schismatic intention, even though one might not formally reject the authority of the Pope or local bishop. Such a position is logically inconsistent, and one must ask what is the prevalent intention in a particular case.

The note points out that one must distinguish between the moral question of the sin of schism, and the legal question of a delict and its imputability. Once there has been an external violation, imputability is presumed until it appears otherwise (Canon 1321, Par. 3). The onus is on the person to establish elements removing or reducing imputability. In the internal forum there is no such presumption. This means that in the case of lay people, their position will often be difficult to discern. In this situation one must have a mind to the liberty guaranteed by Canon 18. In the case of clergy, their external involvement in the ministry in the ambit of the schismatic movement is itself sufficient evidence that both internal and external criteria for formal adherence have been fulfilled. However, such a censure is undeclared and therefore subject to the limits mentioned in Canons 1331 and 1335.

While the document speaks of Lefebvrists, it does not refer by name to the Society of St. Pius X, and so the criteria should be applied also to other similar groups that are associated with the archbishop's followers, religious communities, the dissident clergy of the Diocese of Campos in Brazil, but also others, such as those mentioned above, who hold similar positions, even though their hierarchs may not have been declared excommunicated.

It does not apply to those who belong to groups whose position has been regularized by the Commission Ecclesia Dei, or established by the authority of the local bishop of Scranton on May 24, 1998.

The position of "freelance" clerics, retired or otherwise released from their diocese, but not subject to any other penalty, who are operating chapels without reference to the local bishop, or in defiance of his known wishes would have to be judged on their individual merits. In some cases it may be the bishop rather than the cleric who is not open to dialogue about regularizing their situation in accordance with the provisions of the *motu proprio*. The same may be true for groups of lay people seeking spiritual provision in the form of chaplaincy, and who have availed of the services of a priest or bishop whose situation is irregular.

While there might be a direct approach to the Pontifical Commission Ecclesia Dei, the latter is reluctant to force bishops' hands and prefers to work by persuasion.

July 15, 1998
REV. GORDON F. READ

APPENDIX III

∾

A Word of Caution by
St. Vincent of Lerins (died circa A.D. 450)

"Someone may ask, 'Do heretics also appeal to Scripture?' They do indeed, and with a vengeance; for you may see them scamper through every single book of Holy Scripture — through the books of Moses, the books of Kings, the Psalms, the Epistles, the Gospels, the Prophets. Whether among their own people or among strangers, in private or in public, in speaking or in writing, at convivial meetings or in the streets, hardly ever do they bring forward anything of their own which they do not endeavor to shelter under words of Scripture. Read the works of Paul of Samosata, of Priscillian, of Eunomius, of Jovinian, and the rest of those pests, and you will see an infinite heap of instances, hardly a single page does not bristle with plausible quotations from the New Testament or the Old.

"But the more secretly they conceal themselves under shelter of the divine law, so much the more are they to be feared and guarded against. For they know that the evil stench of their doctrine will hardly find acceptance with any one if it be exhaled pure and simple. They sprinkle it over, therefore, with the perfume of heavenly language, in order that one who would be ready to despise human error, may hesitate to condemn divine words. They do, in fact, what nurses do when they would prepare some bitter draught for children; they smear the edge of the cup all round with honey, that the unsuspecting child, having first tasted the sweet, may have no fear of the bitter. So too do these act, who disguise poisonous herbs and noxious juices under the names of medicines, so that no one almost, when he reads the label, suspects the poison.

"It was for this reason that the Savior cried, 'Beware of false prophets, who come to you in sheep's clothing but inwardly are ravenous wolves' (Matthew 7:15). What is meant by 'sheep's clothing'? What but the words which prophets and apostles with the guilelessness of sheep wove beforehand as fleeces, for that immaculate Lamb which takes away the sin of the world. What are the ravenous wolves? What but the savage and rabid glosses of heretics, who continually infest the Church's folds, and tear in pieces the flock of Christ wherever they are able?

"But that they may with more successful guile steal upon the unsuspecting sheep, retaining the ferocity of the wolf, they put off his appearance, and wrap themselves, so to say, in the language of the divine law, as in a fleece, so that one, having felt the softness of wool, may have no dread of the wolf's fangs. But what sayeth the Savior? 'You will know them by their fruits'(Matthew 7:20). That is, when they have begun not only to quote those divine words, but also to expound them — not as yet only to make a boast of them as on their side, but also to interpret them — then will that bitterness, that acerbity, that rage, be understood; then will the ill-savor of that novel poison be perceived; then will those profane novelties be disclosed; then may you see first the hedge broken through; then the landmarks of the Fathers removed; then the Catholic faith assailed; then the doctrine of the Church torn in pieces" (*The Commonitoria*, 64-66).

Notes

1. The Society of St. Pius X (SSPX) is society of priests and seminarians founded by Archbishop Lefebvre to preserve the pre-Vatican II Liturgy. Soon thereafter, they came to reject the Second Vatican Council. In 1988, the SSPX followed Lefebvre into schism when he consecrated four SSPX priests as bishops without Rome's approval.

2. J. Cardinal Ratzinger, Speech to the Bishops of Chile, 13 July 1988, trans. in Canonical Proposal of the Priestly Fraternity of St. Peter, Scranton, Privately Published, 1993, p. 64.

3. Sedevacantism is the belief that the Chair of Peter has been empty since at least the time of the Second Vatican Council. The term derives from the Latin words *sedes* (chair) and *vacans* (empty). While most sedevacantists uphold Pius XII as the last valid Pope, a minority recognize at least the initial validity of Pope John XXIII's Pontificate.

4. Sedeprivationism is a variation of sedevacantism. It proposes that the post-Vatican II Popes are material, but not formal, successors to St. Peter.

5. CCC = *Catechism of the Catholic Church*

6. Congregation for Bishops, Monitum d.no Marcello Lefebvre, Prot. No. 514/17, 17 June 1988, trans. in *L'Osservatore Romano* (OR), English edition, No. 26, 27 June 1988, p. 2.

7. J. Cardinal Ratzinger, "Telegram to Monsignor Lefebvre," 29 June 1988, in *The Pope Speaks*, 33 (1988), p. 203.

8. D. Oppenheimer, FSSP, *Ecclesia Dei Adflicta: Towards a Deepened Understanding of the Liturgical Value of the Motu Proprio of 2 July 1988*, Rome, Pontifical University of St. Thomas, Faculty of Theology, 1999, p. 80.

9. A. De Castro Mayer, "Declaration," 30 June 1988, in *Is Tradition Excommunicated? Where is Catholicism Today?*, Kansas City, KS, The Angelus Press, 1993, pp. 95-96.

10. Le Crom, *Une Mère de Famille*, Paris, 1948, trans. Mother of a Family: The Life of Madame Gabrielle Lefebvre 1880–1938, Kansas City, KS, Angelus Press, 1994, p. 14.

11. D. Oppenheimer, *Ecclesia Dei Adflicta*, p. 77.

12. B.A. Cathey, "The Legal Background to the Erection and Alleged Suppression of the Society of St. Pius X," in M. Davies, *Apologia Pro Marcel Lefebvre*, Appendix V, p. 443.

13. F. Charrière, Decree Establishing the International Priestly Society of St. Pius X, 1 November 1970, photographically reproduced in M. Davies, *Apologia Pro Marcel Lefebvre*, pp. 102-103, trans. in B. A. Cathey, The Legal Background to the Erection and Alleged Suppression of the Society of St. Pius X, p. 444.

14. Statutes of the Society of St. Pius X, No. 1, as quoted M. Davies, *Apologia Pro Marcel Lefebvre*, p. 443.

15. B.A. Cathey, "The Legal Background to the Erection and Alleged Suppression of the Society of St. Pius X," as quoted in M. Davies, *Apologia Pro Marcel Lefebvre*, p. 444.

16. S. Woywod, OFM, *A Practical Commentary on the Code of Canon Law*, 4th ed., vol. 1, New York, NY, Joseph F. Wagner (Inc.), 1932, par. 578.

17. C. Augustine, OSB, DD, *A Commentary on the New Code of Canon Law*, vol. 3, p. 448.

18. S. Woywod, *A Practical Commentary*, par. 600.

19. Sacred Congregation for the Clergy, Prot. No. 133515/I., 18 Feb. 1971, photographically reproduced in M. Davies, *Apologia Pro Marcel Lefebvre*, pp. 102-103.

20. I.e., suspension from all priestly faculties.

21. M. Lefebvre, SSPX, *An Open Letter to Confused Catholics*, translated by SSPX — Great Britain, Kansas, KS, Angelus Press, 1992, p. 140.

22. D. Oppenheimer, *Ecclesia Dei Adflicta*, p. 78.

23. J. Cardinal Ratzinger and Vitterio Messori, *The Ratzinger Report: An Exclusive Interview on the State of the Church*, translated by S. Attanasio and G. Harrison, San Francisco, CA, Ignatius Press, 1985, p. 33.

24. M. Lefebvre, *La Déclaration du 21 novembre 1974*, 21 November 1974, *Itinéraires*, no. 195, trans. in *The Collected Works of His Excellency Archbishop Marcel Lefebvre*, vol. 1, Dickinson, Texas, The Angelus Press, 1985, p.34.

25. M. Davies, *Apologia Pro Marcel Lefebvre*, p. 43.

26. Ibid., p. 51.

27. S. Woywod, *A Practical Commentary*, par. 594.

28. M. Lefebvre, *An Open Letter to Confused Catholics*, p. 138.

29. S. Woywod, *A Practical Commentary*, par. 372.

30. M. Lefebvre, *An Open Letter to Confused Catholics*, pp. 138-139.

31. Sacred Congregation for Catholic Education, Prot. No. 70/72, 6 May 1975, *Itinéraires*, No. 195, trans. in M. Davies, *Apologia Pro Marcel Lefebvre*, pp. 57-59.

32. F. Charrière, *Decree Establishing the SSPX*, p.444.

33. M. Lefebvre, *La Lettre au cardinal Staffa*, 21 May 1975, *Itinéraires*, n. 195, trans. in M. Davies, *Apologia Pro Marcel Lefebvre*, pp. 73-74.

34. M. Davies, *Apologia Pro Marcel Lefebvre*, p. 106.

35. Paul VI, "Lettre de S. S. Le Pape Paul VI a Mgr. Lefebvre," 29 June 1975, *La Documentation Catholique*, No. 1689, trans. in M. Davies, *Apologia Pro Marcel Lefebvre*, p. 113.

36. S. Woywod, *A Practical Commentary*, vol. 2, par. 1802.

37. H.U. Von Balthasar, *The Office of Peter and the Structure of the Church*, trans. A. Emery, San Francisco, Ignatius Press, 1986, p. 65.

38. M. Davies, *Apologia Pro Marcel Lefebvre*, p. 202.

39. Secretariat of State, Prot. No. 307, 554, 12 June 1976, trans. in M. Davies, *Apologia Pro Marcel Lefebvre*, p. 194.

40. S. Woywod, *A Practical Commentary*, vol. 1, par. 888.

41. Ibid., vol. 2, par. 2229.

42. M. Lefebvre, "Letter to Pope Paul VI," 22 June 1976, trans. in M. Davies, *Apologia Pro Marcel Lefebvre*, p. 196.

43. S. Woywod, *A Practical Commentary*, par. 171.

44. Ibid., par. 909.

45. Secretariat of State, "Letter from Mgr. Benelli to Mgr. Lefebvre," 25 June 1976, trans. in M. Davies, *Apologia Pro Marcel Lefebvre*, p. 197-199

46. S. Woywod, *A Practical Commentary*, par. 15.

47. Cf. Pius V, Bull *Quo Primum Tempore*, 14 July 1570, trans. in M. Davies, *Pope Paul's New Mass*, Kansas City, The Angelus Press, 1992, pp. 531-534.

48. M. Lefebvre, Sermon, 29 June 1976, trans. in M. Davies, *Apologia Pro Marcel Lefebvre*, p. 213.

49. R. Panciroli, Press Conference, 1 July 1976, trans. in M. Davies, *Apologia Pro Marcel Lefebvre*, p. 215.

50. Ibid., p. 216.

51. Sacred Congregation for Bishops, Monition Prot. No. 514/76, 6 July 1976, trans. in M. Davies, *Apologia Pro Marcel Lefebvre*, pp. 225-226.

52. R. Panciroli, Press Conference, p. 216

53. Sacred Congregation for Bishops, Prot. No. 514/76, p. 226.

54. Sacred Congregation for Bishops, Notification of Supension sion *a Divinis*, Prot. No. 514/76, 22 July 1976, trans. in M. Davies, *Apologia Pro Marcel Lefebvre*, p. 235.

55. S. Woywod, *A Practical Commentary*, vol. 2, par. 2184.

56. M. Lefebvre, *Lettre de Mgr. Lefebvre a Paul VI* 17 June 1976, *La Documentation Catholique*, n. 1705, trans. in M. Davies, *Apologia Pro Marcel Lefebvre*, p. 234.

57. Sacred Congregation for Bishops, Notification of Supension sion, pp.235-236.

58. S. Woywod, *A Practical Commentary*, vol. 2, par. 2121.

59. John Paul II, Motu proprio *Ecclesia Dei*, p. 150.

60. G. Potter, *After the Boston Heresy Case*, Monrovia, Catholic Treasures Books, 1995, p. 181.

61. Ibid., p. 180.

62. C.P. Nemeth, *The Case of Archbishop Marcel Lefebvre; Trial by Canon Law*, Kansas City, Angelus Press, 1994, p. 92.

63. Ibid., p. 97.

64. Pontifical Council for the Interpretation of Legislative Texts, *Nota sulla scommunica per scisma in cui incorrono gli aderenti al movimento del Vescovo Marcel Lefebvre*, allegato al Prot. No. Protocol 5233/9624 August 1996, *Communicationes*, 29(2) [1997], trans. The Canon Law Society of Great Britain and Ireland (16 March 1999). See full text in Appendix II of this book.

65. *Suprema Sacra Congregatio S. Officii, Decretum de consecratione episcopi sine canonica provisione*, 9 April 1951, *AAS*, 43 [1951], p. 217-218.

66. T.C.G. Glover, *Schism and Archbishop Lefebvre*, p. 104.

67. Ibid., p. 104.

68. Romans 13:1-2.

69. Cf. Fr. Gérald Beauchamp de Servigny, "Was Vatican II Merely a Pastoral Council?," translated by Pete Vere, *Envoy Magazine*, Vol. 7, No. 3, pp. 24-29.

70. John XXIII, 11 October 1962, translated by Pete Vere

71. Yves Congar, *Entretiens d'automne*, Cerf, Paris, 1987, p. 13.

72. Paul VI, Letter to Archbishop Lefebvre, Nov. 10, 1976.

73. Congar, *Entretiens d'automne*, op cit. p. 10.

74. Cf. paragraph 38 of *Gaudium et Spes*, the Second Vatican Council's Pastoral Constitution of the Church: "The Lord left behind a pledge of this hope and strength for life's journey in that sacrament of faith where natural elements refined by man are changed into His glorified Body and Blood, providing a meal of brotherly solidarity and a foretaste of the heavenly banquet."

75. Second Vatican Council, *Unitatis Redintegratio*, Decree on Ecumenism, Par. 2.

76. Cf. Patrick Madrid, *Pope Fiction*, San Diego, Basilica Press, 1999, pp. 141-147.

77. The expression "wide and generous," commonly quoted in English translations of *Ecclesia Dei*, is actually a mistranslation of the official Latin text. For more information on this controversy, please see Fr. William Woestman's article "Reflection on *Ecclesia Dei* and Its Translations," in *Monitor Ecclesiasticus*, 116 (1991), pp. 483-487.

Glossary of Ecclesiastical Terms

Anathema: A formal condemnation by the Church of a certain moral or theological position as contrary to Catholic faith and morals.

Canon law: The Church's internal legal system, in both its implementation and interpretation. Canon law allows the Church to function smoothly in carrying out her work of saving souls.

Censure: Another name for a medicinal penalty, or a penalty intended to help the offender repent and return to the heart of the Church. The *Code of Canon Law* presently contains three censures: suspension, interdict, and excommunication.

CIEL: French acronym for the "International Center of Liturgical Study." Ciel is also the French word for "heaven." One of the most dynamic lay initiatives to arise from the *Ecclesia Dei* movement, CIEL is a group of young intellectuals seeking to promote non-polemical academic dialogue on the 1962 Liturgy, while strengthening the traditionalist movement's foundation in the Second Vatican Council, fidelity to the Holy See and diocesan bishops, and communion with the rest of the

Church. CIEL has national delegations from various countries around the world.

Code of Canon Law: A legal compilation of seven books that contain the basic laws of the Latin Church. (Eastern Catholics have their own *Code of Canons of the Eastern Churches*.) The seven books are as follows: General Norms; People of God; The Teaching Office of the Church; The Sanctifying Office of the Church; Temporal Goods; Penal Law; and Procedural Law.

Custom: A common practice arising within a church community that through constant repetition becomes the law within that community, even if the custom is not written down anywhere. Canon law holds that custom is the best interpreter of the law. For example, it is the custom in some parishes to kneel for consecration before the Sanctus, whereas it is the custom in other parishes to kneel after the Sanctus.

Declare sentence: A public declaration by the competent Church authority that someone has incurred an automatic penalty according to canon law. This is different from an imposed penalty, in which a judge imposes a penalty after a Church trial.

Discipline of the Faith: A practice of the faith that is not of itself doctrinal, but is meant to help us observe the Church's teaching. In other words, it is something the Church asks us to do in order to help us focus on God's commandments.

Ecclesia Dei: (See Appendix I) Pope John Paul II's 1988 *moto proprio* declaring Archbishop Lefebvre and those who adhere to his schism excommunicated. In order to help reconcile the traditionalists with the Church, this document also expands permission for each individual bishop to allow the sacraments within his diocese to be celebrated according to the 1962 liturgical missal.

Ecclesia Dei **movement:** A movement in full communion with the Roman Pontiff and the Catholic Church that adheres to the 1962 liturgical Missal according to the special permission granted by Pope John Paul II in *Ecclesia Dei.*

Episcopus vagus: A wandering bishop not recognized by the Church, or a bishop who claims an official title not recognized by the Church.

Excommunication: The Church's highest censure or medicinal penalty, in which the offender is completely cut off from the daily life of the Church, including sacraments.

Excommunication *ferendae sententiae*: An excommunication imposed as the result of a judgment of a Church tribunal.

Excommunication *latae sententiae* **reserved to the Apostolic See:** An automatic excommunication (*latae sententiae*) that only the Roman Pontiff and his Roman Congregations can remove (thus "reserved to the Apostolic See").

Expiatory penalty: A penalty imposed as a penance, in order to help the offender repair the damage he has done. For example, a Catholic doctor who has repented of the crime of abortion, and had his excommunication removed by the diocesan bishop, may be asked to read Pope Paul VI's papal encyclical *Humanae Vitae* as an expiatory penalty.

Faculty: The power and permission from the Church to carry out certain acts, such as hearing confessions.

Ferendae sententiae: A penalty imposed after a Church trial in which the offender has been judged guilty of some crime.

General Norms: The first book of the *Code of Canon Law*, which contains all the basic legal principles through which the rest of canon law is interpreted. For example, Canon 18 is a general norm stating that in the interpretation of canon law, those laws that give us favors are to include as many cases as possible, whereas laws that punish us are to include as few cases as possible.

Indult Mass: A Mass offered according to the 1962 Liturgical Missal with the permission of the legitimate diocesan bishop by a priest in full communion with Rome.

Jurisdiction: The power to carry out certain acts of governance among a portion of Christ's faithful. For example, a priest has the jurisdiction to marry people in his parish, but needs the permission of the pastor in a parish across town before marrying people in that parish.

Latae sententiae: An automatic penalty imposed by virtue of the law. For example, a Catholic doctor who performs an abortion is excommunicated *latae sententiae* under canon law. So long as it is publicly proven he performed an abortion and has not repented, a bishop can simply declare the sentence of excommunication without going through the process of a Church trial.

Latin Church *sui iuris*: Formerly known as Latin Rite Catholics, the Latin Church *sui iuris* is composed of those Catholics who descend from the Catholic Church in the West, as opposed to the Christian East. For example, a Melkite Catholic would belong to the Melkite Church *sui iuris*. The Roman Catholic Church is composed of twenty-two Churches *sui iuris*.

Legislate: To pass a law with the intention of binding the faithful to that law.

Licit/illicit status: The lawfulness or unlawfulness of a certain act that may or may not affect the validity of that act. For example, an SSPX priest says Mass illicitly because, according to the Catholic Church, it is unlawful for him to say Mass. However, his Mass is still valid because the bread and wine are transubstantiated into the Body, Blood, Soul, and Divinity of Jesus Christ when he says the words of consecration.

Medicinal penalty: A penalty not so much intended to punish the offender as to force him to repent and be restored to the Church. For example, a Catholic doctor who commits an abortion is excommunicated in order to force him to repent of his crime. Once he is truly repentant, he has the right to have the excommunication lifted. The ordinary may then impose an expiatory penalty.

Mere ecclesiastical law: A law of the Church that is only disciplinary in nature and thus can be changed or dispensed with in order to meet the needs of the Church. For example, the law that a Catholic cannot marry a catechumen is merely an ecclesiastical law. The bishop can dispense from this law for a good reason.

***Mystici Corporis*:** Pope Pius XII's papal encyclical on the Church as the mystical body of Christ.

***Novus Ordo Missae*:** The liturgical missal revised by Pope Paul VI after the Second Vatican Council, which is presently used in the Latin Church *sui iuris*.

Papal mandate: The approval given by the Roman Pontiff to a bishop in order to licitly consecrate another bishop.

Penalty: A punishment given by the legitimate Church authority to someone who acts contrary to canon law.

Priestly Fraternity of St. Peter (FSSP): A society of apostolic life, similar to a religious order, composed of priests who have been entrusted by Pope John Paul II with the apostolate of ministering the sacraments to Catholics according to the 1962 liturgical missal. It is the largest and best-known priestly institute to arise out of the *Ecclesia Dei* movement.

Promulgate: To put forward a new law or teaching within the Church.

Quo Primum Tempore: St. Pius V's papal bull codifying the Latin Liturgy around the time of the Council of Trent.

Roman Pontiff: The Bishop of Rome, who occupies the see founded by St. Peter and St. Paul, and who succeeds St. Peter as visible head of the Church. "You mean the Pope?" Not necessarily, because St. Peter founded the See of Antioch before coming to Rome, and thus, traditionally, some of the Eastern Patriarchs also legitimately claim the title "Pope." However, there is only one Roman Pontiff in the Church at any given time.

Schism: To break communion with or refuse to subject oneself to the Roman Pontiff or the Church in communion with him.

State of necessity: An emergency situation in which canon law no longer applies because of a greater need for the good of souls. For example, because of Communist persecution in China, a bishop there can ordain a seminarian to the priesthood without requiring that he first finish all of his seminary studies.

Subjection to the Roman Pontiff: To submit oneself in obedience to the teaching and discipline of the Bishop of Rome.

Supplied jurisdiction: An emergency or unknown situation in which the Church provides jurisdiction where it would otherwise be lacking due to unforeseen circumstances. For example, a newly ordained priest lacks the faculty to hear confessions because he hasn't passed his jurisdiction exam yet. Suppose that on his way to his jurisdiction exam he comes across a car accident in which a Catholic is seriously injured. The Church would supply this newly ordained priest with jurisdiction to hear the dying Catholic's confession.

Supreme legislator: The Roman Pontiff, when he's using his authority to legislate or interpret canon law.

Suspension: A censure of a cleric in which his rights, obligations, and faculties arising from holy orders are removed. For example, a suspended priest is no longer permitted to celebrate Mass or hear confessions.

Tradition: The Deposit of Faith left by Christ and His Apostles which has been passed down to us through the Church, whose job it is to mediate and interpret it for the faithful.

Traditional Mass: A Mass offered according to the 1962 liturgical missal, the last liturgical missal before the reforms of Pope Paul VI.

Traditionalist movement: A movement seeking to preserve, and in some cases completely restore, the Tridentine Mass within the Latin Church *sui iuris*. It is divided into various camps, both inside and outside the Catholic Church.

ιe **Mass:** Another commonly used name for Mass cel-
:cording to the 1962 Missal which, apart from some
minor changes, closely resembles the liturgical missal codified
by Pope St. Pius V around the time of the Council of Trent in
the sixteenth century.

Valid/invalid status: Validity determines the effectiveness of the
act one is attempting to carry out, regardless of whether such
an act is licit or illicit (canonically legal or illegal). For example, we've already noted that a Mass is valid when said by an
SSPX priest, although illicit. However, if a layman were to
dress up as a priest and attempt to celebrate Mass in public,
such a Mass would be not only illicit, but invalid as well — it
would lack the effects of a true Mass. This is because a non-
ordained person cannot transubstantiate the bread and wine
into the Body, Blood, Soul, and Divinity of our Lord Jesus
Christ.

About the Authors

PATRICK MADRID and his wife Nancy have been married for 24 years and have been blessed by God with eleven healthy and happy children. A cradle Catholic, Patrick has been active in the field of Catholic apologetics since the 1980s.

As an author, his books include *Where Is That In the Bible?*, *Why Is That In Tradition?*, *Answer Me This!*, *Pope Fiction*, *Search and Rescue*, *Any Friend of God's Is a Friend of Mine*, and the best-selling, multi-volume *Surprised by Truth* series (with over 400,000 copies sold).

Patrick is also the host of several EWTN television and radio programs, including "Search and Rescue," "Pope Fiction," "The Truth About Scripture and Tradition," and "Where Is That In the Bible?"

At the invitation of many bishops, priests, and lay groups, he has conducted hundreds of seminars and conferences at parishes and universities across the United States, as well as in Canada, throughout Europe, and in Latin America, Asia, Australia, and New Zealand. For more information about Patrick's work, including details on how to schedule him to speak at your parish, please visit his website: www.surprisedbytruth.com.

PETE VERE and his wife Sonya just celebrated their fourth wedding anniversary. They are the proud parents of two young daughters. Pete grew up in northern Ontario, obtained a licentiate in canon law from St. Paul University in Ottawa, Canada, and he is now back at his alma mater pursuing a civil and ecclesiastical doctorate in canon law.

His writings on canon law have been published in *Envoy*, *The Wanderer*, *Roman Replies & CLSA Advisory Opinions*, *The Catholic Answer*, *Challenge*, *Homiletic & Pastoral Review*, *The Interim*, *Bread of Life*, and *Enter Stage Right*. His reversion story from the SSPX schism appears in *Surprised by Truth 3*.

His journey into Catholic apologetics began shortly after he left the SSPX. At the invitation of Bill Grossklas, Pete began writing for *Agenda* — a newsletter and website Bill published for former SSPX adherents. Along with fellow regular contributors Shawn McElhinney and John Loughnan, Pete spent many formative years at *Agenda* as together this foursome researched and refuted several arguments put forward by schismatic traditionalists.

In November of 2002, Pete joined with several other Canadian Catholic apologists to co-found Catholic-Legate.com. This website has now grown into Canada's largest apostolate dedicated to Catholic apologetics. Pete also serves as an International Director with the Order of Alhambra — a 100-year-old Catholic family organization dedicated to assisting the mentally and cognitively challenged.

Our Sunday Visitor ...
Your Source for Discovering
the Riches of the Catholic Faith

Our Sunday Visitor has an extensive line of materials for young children, teens, and adults. Our books, Bibles, pamphlets, CD-ROMs, audios, and videos are available in bookstores worldwide.

To receive a FREE full-line catalog or for more information, call **Our Sunday Visitor** at **1-800-348-2440, ext. 3**. Or write **Our Sunday Visitor** / 200 Noll Plaza / Huntington, IN 46750.

Please send me ____ A catalog
Please send me materials on:
____ Apologetics and catechetics
____ Prayer books
____ The family
____ Reference works
____ Heritage and the saints
____ The parish

Name _____
Address _____ Apt._____
City _____ State _____ Zip_____
Telephone ( ) _____
                                                        A39BBBBP

Please send a friend ____ A catalog
Please send a friend materials on:
____ Apologetics and catechetics
____ Prayer books
____ The family
____ Reference works
____ Heritage and the saints
____ The parish

Name _____
Address _____ Apt._____
City _____ State _____ Zip_____
Telephone ( ) _____
                                                        A49BBDBP

OurSundayVisitor

200 Noll Plaza, Huntington, IN 46750
Toll free: **1-800-348-2440**
Website: www.osv.com